"We lo ... tic,
even li ... oth
challer ... eds
or old ... this
wonde ... We
are ex ... ; in
greate ...

... dox
Inn

"I wou ... o-be
marri ... fall,
reden ... rsical
sexua ... In a
cultu ... , it is
an er ... nacy,
selfle

PATF ... ector,
(... ydney

"Adri ... k and
answ ... imacy
in C ... iblical
and (therefore) practical, and which any couple ... of their
married life would find helpful to review regularly. This is a book
that is enjoyable to read and enjoyable to put into practice."

PHILIP MOORE Network Director, ACTS 29 Europe

"Adrian and Celia have done a great job with *Closer*: a br...
realistic book, refreshingly honest and ... the b...
within marriage. Giving clear gospel fou ...
encourage and help couples to commu...
the big questions. We found the emph...
the reminder that the pursuit of a godly ...

of holiness especially helpful. Having counselled countless numbers of couples over the past 20 years, we know that this is a much needed book that we will be encouraging every married couple in our church to read."   STEVE AND SIAN ROBINSON

Steve is the Pastor of Cornerstone Church, Liverpool, UK

"This refreshingly frank book is cleverly written so as to be informative without being embarrassing. Thoroughly biblical, highly accessible, with principles that will be relevant for couples whatever stage they are at. Fantastic as a resource for marriage prep—or for any marriages looking to explore God's design for intimacy."

JONTY AND LINDA ALLCOCK

Jonty is the Pastor of The Globe Church, London
Linda is the author of *Deeper Still*

"Adrian and Celia have written a little book on a big subject. Over the last two decades, as we have invested in our marriage and in Christian ministry, we have faced many situations ourselves and have seen many couples around us struggling with intimacy. We believe that to have at hand this honest and very personal yet deeply biblical treatment on this much needed topic will help many and will bring blessing and joy to couples who want to glorify God in every area of their lives."

BEN AND HENI UHRIN

Ben is President of the Slovak Baptist Union

"Too often sex is either addressed spiritually without acknowledging the realities of life or it's over simplified as if we should all have it figured out by now. Despite the challenge, Adrian and Celia have beautifully interwoven the wonder of God's gift and design with being practical about the challenges and questions bombarding us— giving us a higher view of what being closer is really about."

JEFF AND SARAH WALTON

Authors, *Together Through the Storms*

Closer

Adrian and
Celia Reynolds

thegoodbook
COMPANY

Closer
A realistic book about intimacy for Christian marriages
© Adrian Reynolds and Celia Reynolds, 2021

Published by:
The Good Book Company

thegoodbook.com | thegoodbook.co.uk
thegoodbook.com.au | thegoodbook.co.nz | thegoodbook.co.in

Cover design by ninefootone creative | Art direction and diagrams by André Parker

ISBN: 9781784985738 | Printed in the UK

CONTENTS

SECTION 1

The beginning

How would you complete the following sentence?
In the beginning…

You might be someone who knows your Bible well, in which case you would perhaps complete the sentence the way the Old Testament does in Genesis—"In the beginning God created the heavens and the earth". Or maybe you thought of the New Testament wording from the start of John's Gospel—"In the beginning was the Word…"? Full marks.

But you might take a more philosophical approach. *In the beginning there was nothing,* you could reply. You would also score highly. God made all things out of nothing (Hebrews 11 v 3), so considered from this angle, this answer is also right.

Or maybe you are more theological in your thinking (and, let's be honest, just a little abstract). *In the beginning, God.* That's your answer. Just, "God". Period. Full stop. Your science teacher might not score this an A+, but your religious studies or philosophy teacher might award the top grade. Right again.

But seeing as this is a book about sex, let us suggest another way to complete the sentence.

In the beginning, *God thought of sex.*

We doubt you'd ever complete the sentence this way. Indeed, you might think that such a sentence is bordering on blasphemy, or at the very least, it's pushing the boundaries a little. But that kind of response reveals precisely the problem that many Christians have about sex. Married believers know sex is enjoyable, fun, intimate, delightful: but they can't quite bring themselves to include it in a list of holy disciplines.

Couples should pray. And read their Bibles. And belong to a church. And be hospitable. And be godly. And all of these in increasing measure, or at least with increasing delight and skill. And to this list, we want to add delight in one another and in the sexual union that God has gifted you. It's why we've written this book.

For in the beginning, *God thought of sex.*

IT BEGAN SO WELL

The first two chapters of the Bible describe God's "very good" creation. After each day of creation activity, readers are greeted with the same refrain: "And God saw that it was good". Then, at the end of day six, when God creates the land-based animals and man and woman, the refrain alters a little. It becomes "God saw all that he had made, and it was *very* good" (Genesis 1 v 31).

This is his divine verdict on creation. It is perfect in every way—fit for the purpose for which he had made it. No sin. No evil. No death. No pandemics. No environmental disasters. And this perfection was in the bedroom too. No selfish motives. No pain. No frustration. No rape. No sexual assault. Just perfect.

The pinnacle of this perfection was the creation of man and woman themselves. We should not separate them out from the rest of creation entirely; they form—together with the entire world—part of God's universal creating prowess. Adam and Eve are made from the same material as the animal kingdom (compare Genesis 1 v 24 with 2 v 7). Nevertheless, it is impossible to read these opening chapters of the Bible and not realise that humankind is something special.

Only humankind is made in God's image (Genesis 1 v 27). Only humankind is addressed directly (Genesis 1 v 28). Only humankind has the actual breath of God within them (Genesis 2 v 7). And this specialness is exemplified in the role that God gives to his first people.

It is summarised in verse 28 of the first chapter: "God blessed them and said to them, 'Be fruitful and increase in number; fill the earth and subdue it. Rule over the fish in the sea and the birds in the sky and over every living creature that moves on the ground.'"

At first glance this creation mandate (as it is sometimes called) seems to have two elements. One is procreation: "Be fruitful and increase in number". The second is to "rule over" creation. While it may sometimes be useful to consider them separately, it should be pretty obvious that they are not entirely distinct.

For the world of God's creating power is a big place. There are lots of animals. Lots of birds. Lots of fields to plough. Lots of lakes to fish, and so on. Adam and Eve may be the first of humankind, but if they are going to fulfil the command to rule over "every living creature" they are certainly not going to be able to do it alone. Hence the first part of the mandate: "Be fruitful and increase in number".

And how are they to do this? The answer is, of course, sex. Martin Luther, the German reformer, famously quipped that if he had been planning things he would have gone for the easier approach of bringing people into the world the same way God did—through forming them from the ground. But he was also the first to acknowledge that he was not the Great Planner. God was, and is. And his perfect plan was for Adam and Eve to make love and make babies.

In the beginning, *God thought of sex.*

THINK BIG

However, when seen in the whole sweep of the Scriptures, Genesis 1 – 2 presents a picture of sexual union which is even more profound than this. Read on to the end of chapter 2 and its retelling of the creation account. Once man and woman are created, and Adam has sung the first recorded chart topper to his new love (v 23), the chapter closes with a remarkable statement:

> *That is why a man leaves a father and mother and is united to his wife, and they become one flesh. Adam and his wife were both naked, and they felt no shame.*   v 24-25

Here is the first marriage and the author deliberately takes Adam and Eve's story and makes it our own. We know he is doing this because the first sentence doesn't actually describe Adam's situation precisely: he has no father and mother to leave. Rather, the narrative takes Adam and Eve and appropriates their story to the whole of history. This verse is for all who will come in their line. It's for us.

In their union, God establishes (still as part of his perfect creation, note) a pattern for all time. This union is a "one-flesh" union. Our minds might immediately jump to sex when we read this phrase, but in fact it describes something more profound than even the act of a husband and wife sleeping together. After all, if a couple cannot enjoy sexual intimacy for a season (for example because of illness) it does not stop them being a one-flesh unit. However, it would also be true to say that nothing expresses this oneness like sex does.

If you are married (and we're assuming that most people reading this book are), you know this is true. Think of all the things you like doing together: sharing a glass of wine over a cosy dinner, perhaps; screaming together for your team at a sports event, or singing along with your favourite band at a live gig; having a great holiday experience. All good. But none of them (or anything else you could think of) really expresses "two becoming one" like sexual intimacy can and does, either physically or emotionally.

So far so good. But there is more. For as the Bible story unfolds, we discover that this one-flesh union of a man and a woman, joined together in marriage, and consummated and enjoyed in the bedroom, is itself a picture of something even greater. Whether it is in the pictures of the Old Testament or the explicit teaching of the New, the Holy Spirit inspired Bible writers to see this joining together as a picture of the eternal and pure relationship between Christ and his church, the Saviour and his beloved, the Bridegroom and his bride.

Take just one place—Paul's letter to the Ephesians:

> *Husbands, love your wives, just as Christ loved the church and gave himself up for her to make her holy, cleansing her by the washing with water through the word, and to present her to himself as a radiant church, without stain or wrinkle or any other blemish, but holy and blameless. In this same way, husbands ought to love their wives as their own bodies. He who loves his wife loves himself. After all, no one ever hated their own body, but they feed and care for their body, just as Christ does the church—for we are members of his body. "For this reason a man will leave his father and mother and be united to his wife, and the two will become one flesh." This is a profound mystery—but I am talking about Christ and the church.*
>
> Ephesians 5 v 25-32

The apostle Paul quotes this very verse from Genesis to make—initially—a point about how husbands are to love their wives. But in so doing, he seamlessly moves into a more profound point: that at its root, marriage is itself a picture of a deeper relationship—"Christ and the church".

The Church of England *Book of Common Prayer* marriage

service—in words which date back to 1549—recognises this connection and makes it explicit in the famous words read out at countless weddings:

> *Dearly beloved, we are gathered together here in the sight of God, and in the face of this Congregation, to join together this man and this woman in holy Matrimony; which is an honourable estate, instituted of God in the time of man's innocency, signifying unto us the mystical union that is betwixt Christ and his Church.*

TAKE ME TO HEAVEN

What this means for married couples is simple. Our marriages themselves reflect a deeper truth than two loving individuals brought together for a lifetime: they reflect the one-flesh union between Christ and his church. And just as sexual intimacy is the deepest *experience* of our earthly one-flesh union, so it must follow that our sexual intimacy is the deepest *reflection* of the extraordinary oneness that being joined to Christ brings.

It is more than making babies; it is making a point.

All of this means that sex, in its proper context, is holy. Not only is it part of God's very good creation, but it reflects the purest and deepest relationship any human can experience: that of being part of Christ's bride, joined to him for all eternity. Sex is many things, as you will no doubt know! It is fun, it is frustrating. It is messy, it is joyful. It is funny (sometimes!), it is consoling. But above all, it is holy. By that we mean that God sets it apart as a gift to married couples to serve him as we seek the good of one another.

The historian Tom Holland recognises this in his recent bestseller *Dominion*, a book which charts the influence of Christianity upon the world. He writes that in this holy understanding of marriage...

> ... *was another marker of the revolution that Christianity had brought to the erotic. The insistence of Scripture that a man and woman, whenever they took to the marital bed, were joined as Christ and his Church were joined, becoming one flesh, gave to both a rare dignity.*

Or, as one of our friends put it in a slightly more down-to-earth way, when a husband or wife invites their spouse to "Take me to heaven, darling!" they are speaking much better than they know.

The story of sex does not end with Genesis 2, however.

If only it did.

Instead, things now take a turn for the worse.

MUCH WORSE

It is impossible to think of the goodness of sexual intimacy without also contemplating its corruption. There is joy in the bedroom, but there is also frustration. There is selfless devotion, but there is also self-absorbed fantasy. There is mutual serving, but there is also rape and assault. There is freely giving oneself, but there is also sexual blackmail. And so the list goes on.

All of this corruption can be traced back to one chapter of the Bible—Genesis 3. Theologian and author Don Carson says that to truly understand humanity's issues, we need to understand humanity's root problem—and according to Genesis 3, that problem is a rejection of God, his good rule and his gracious plan.

It doesn't take long for Adam and Eve to assert their independence from God and pay the consequences. This third chapter of the Bible tells their sorry tale which is the story we all share. In essence, it is the story of the first couple seeing themselves in place of God and paying the price. Their rebellion against their Creator and rejection of his one rule for the garden draws his swift and righteous justice, what we sometimes call "the curse".

The curse affects every element of the creation mandate. Verses 15 and 16 of chapter 3 directly impact both the command to be fruitful (for childbearing will be a painful process) and the command to rule together (for both man and woman will now be in confused conflict).

Moreover, the very nature of the work of ruling that they are given to do will be affected. "Cursed is the ground because of you" (v 17). The creation mandate is not removed. But it is made much more difficult because of sin. It should not surprise us therefore that sin affects sex, given that we have seen how integral sex is to God's very good creation. Each of us sees how comprehensive this impact is.

For example, we know that, although there is lots of sex

around, not all of it is holy. Context counts for a lot. In a marriage relationship, between a man and a woman, sex is sanctified, though sin can still make it unholy. Outside of this relationship, it is *never* holy; it is quite the opposite, in fact. For it neither reflects the creation setting that God has given, nor pictures the exclusive relationship Christ has with his church.

As our friend Sam Allberry writes in his excellent book *Why Does God Care Who I Sleep With?*, "Like any powerful force, it needs to be used rightly, which means being used in the right setting". We should not think this is an odd concept. There are plenty of examples of how the setting makes all the difference.

Consider driving a car. If we told you that we were driving at 65 mph, you would need to know a little more before you knew if we were driving carefully and legally, or not. If the journey was on a fast road with a 70 mph limit, you would consider that to be careful, safe driving. If, instead, it was past a school with a 20 mph limit, you would consider that to be the height of recklessness, and we would be fully deserving of the firm hand of the law.

And so it is with sex. Context is everything. And what is holy and good and wholesome in marriage, is equally unholy and damaging outside of it. As couples come to recognise this distinction, they can find that past sinful experiences hold them back in their marriages. As this is such an important issue to address, and possibly one that you personally are wrestling with, we have written specifically about two aspects of it in the supplementary chapters at the end.

Even if this is not your experience, every couple also feels the effects of the fall on their own sexual relationship. This is the closer-to-home-application of the reality of Genesis 3. Sometimes, theologians talk about the doctrine of "total depravity": not that everything is as bad as it could be (it is patently not), but that everything we think and do is affected by sin to some extent.

You feel this in the bedroom. We know you do, because we do, and everyone we have spoken to does as well. Motives, thoughts, actions and the ability of our bodies to function the way we want them to—all are affected by sin. So sexual fulfilment is affected directly. Some of these sins are obvious. Some are hidden (such as a wandering imagination).

All of this is a world away from "naked, and they felt no shame" (Genesis 2 v 25). We all want that experience. We all long for honesty, closeness, the exquisite delight of being seen, appreciated, accepted and cherished for what we are. Yet we also want to cover up, push people away and turn off the light, because sin permeates every fibre of our being. That tension between 'close but not too close' in even the best of marriages is a constant reminder that brokenness is in the world.

Moreover, the infection of sin also has an indirect impact. Even when there is no direct causation, sickness is in the world because sin is. It's not usually right to make direct links between sin and individual illnesses we might suffer from— Jesus certainly does not (see John 9 v 1-3, for example). But in the Bible's big picture, sickness is an alien invader into God's perfect world. The response "not tonight, I have a headache" is also ultimately a consequence of Genesis 3.

In his book, *The Genesis of Sex*, O. Palmer Robertson points out how the fall, and the sin that results, leads to a dramatic corruption of God's plan for intimacy in just the first book of the Bible. He shows how "carelessness, lust, adultery, rape, incest and homosexuality" all flow from Adam and Eve's first fall from grace within just a few generations. We should not be surprised when we see the same drama playing out in our own lives and the lives of those around us. Only saddened.

THINGS CAN ONLY GET BETTER. AND BETTER.

But we are not without hope. For we know that in the Bible story creation and the fall are followed by redemption. It is the gospel which gives Christians hope. This gospel is the good news that God himself, in the person of Jesus, has entered into the broken world in order to rescue us, and it. In Jesus who died and rose again there is both forgiveness and power to change. Our sin is no longer counted against us; nor is it our master. As the old hymn writer Charles Wesley so succinctly and memorably puts it, "He breaks the power of cancelled sin".

And this glorious gospel affects all of life. We are not just spiritual beings, transformed by faith in Christ on the inside only: we all have experienced and continue to pray for external transformation too.

Take our speech for example. We know that without Christ and his indwelling Spirit, our words, like every other part of our being, are tainted by sin. We don't always tell the truth. We speak rashly. We lose our tempers.. We gossip. But we hope and expect that the gospel will change us. We don't expect to carry on with the same sinful speech and we're frustrated when these old patterns of behaviour creep through.

It's just the same when it comes to sexual intimacy. We should expect redemption to make a difference to us in the bedroom as much as it does on the twitter feed. In fact, we often tell people that when it comes to sex, Christians should be joyful optimists. They should not only treasure and enjoy sex, recognising its place in God's economy; they should also pray, hope and trust for it to become ever more sanctified. More of this shortly.

Redemption is not the end of the matter, however. In the pattern of Scripture, creation-fall-redemption is followed by consummation. For Christians, we should expect better in this life as the Spirit transforms us. And we should expect *much* better as we await the most glorious of hopes: "Just as we have borne the image of the earthly man, so shall we bear the image of the heavenly man" (1 Corinthians 15 v 49). Better, yes. And one day, much better.

We realise that any talk of consummation in a book about sex runs the risk of being seriously misunderstood! For the purposes of being absolutely clear, we are not talking about sexual consummation here: the initial joining together of a husband and wife, thankfully not in today's society an event requiring witnesses (though it has in times past).

Spiritual consummation is quite a different thing. It reflects that the whole of human history is headed somewhere. God's plan is to bring things to a glorious climax (if you'll excuse the pun). The apostle Paul explains this in the same section of Ephesians that we considered earlier. This climax will be the full and final joining together of Christ the Bridegroom with the church his bride: "to present her to himself as a radiant church, without stain or wrinkle or any other blemish, but holy and blameless" (Ephesians 5 v 27).

And when this glorious consummation takes place, there will no longer be any need for the earthly picture God has given us now. There will be no marriage in heaven because we will have the greater reality to which it points. There will be no sexual intimacy in heaven because every believer—whatever their marital state on earth—will experience in every single moment the perfect and indescribable joy of being joined intimately to their Saviour.

All of which gives Christians a good and right perspective on sex. It is a temporary joy before the eternal reality takes over. As another of our friends, pastor and author Christopher Ash, puts it, "Sex is not *ultimately* important. But it is *jolly* important". Maybe for the moment we could all echo the Kane Gang's 1980s classic: "This could be the closest thing to heaven I have ever known". But that's not a song we'll be singing when Jesus returns. We'll have no need.

All of this puts us at odds with the world. When we first wrote about sex, we sent a copy of what we had prepared to Suzi Godson. Suzi is one of the UK's foremost sexual counsellors, author of many books and countless articles. We have always liked her writing, valuing—as she seems to do—many of the same things we value: patience, commitment, selflessness and so on. She kindly read what we had written and wrote us a short note in return. "I wish you well with your book", she wrote, "but you clearly have a completely different view of sex from me."

At first, we were a little annoyed. Was the outworking of our view really so different? Yet as we reflected on her response, we realised she was exactly right, for in all the common ground on behaviour, communication and resolution that we shared, Suzi would never be able to say the one thing that we believe is a prerequisite to any Christian discussion about making love:

In the beginning, *God thought of sex.*

THE TALK

T alking about sex seems a bit weird. Embarrassing perhaps. Certainly private. "None of your business" is the phrase that would spring to many minds; perhaps yours.

But it's a talk we need to have.

Our memories of having "the birds and bees talk" with our own parents as we were growing up are rather hazy and affected by the long period of time that has passed and the acute sense of embarrassment we both felt. Neither of us remember it being particularly helpful and—in one case—it seems looking back that the explanation was physiologically impossible. In a similar vein, one of our extended family remembers shutting herself in a cupboard because she was so mortified at what her mother was telling her. You may have similar stories.

The expression "birds and bees", when you stop to think about it, is an odd one. Birds, as you may remember from school biology classes, mate by rubbing their cloaca together. Male bees on the other hand leave parts of their genitals behind. It's hardly a helpful way of introducing sex. And the trouble with these little chats is that they rarely get to the important themes we've been discovering in the pages of the Bible.

Even more significantly, we tend to think of "the talk" as a one-off opportunity. Overwhelmed with embarrassment, parents gear themselves up for the chat and then breathe a deep sigh of relief when the moment is over—whether or not it ends up with someone locking themselves in the cupboard.

A healthy, godly view of sex, however, is more than a simple outline of the "what" and "how" of most parent-children conversations. In fact, we would argue, for most Christian parents, the priority should not be what sex *involves* so much as what it *signifies*. We need to talk to our children, if we have them, about *meaning* alongside *mechanics*. We need to extol holiness alongside warnings against sin.

Most importantly, we need to talk about what it means to grow in our holiness in this area—what the Bible calls sanctification.

WHAT MAKES SEX "BETTER"?

In every other area of our Christian lives, we believe it is both possible and desirable to increase in holiness. We can't presume on such growth, nor is it ever easy. But growth in godliness is a key mark of a healthy believer. This is the work that God himself does in us. "And we all ... are being transformed into his image with ever-increasing glory, which comes from the

Lord, who is the Spirit," writes Paul (2 Corinthians 3 v 18). Not only so, but we can be confident in God's commitment to this great cause, as the same apostle writes to the Philippian believers, "He who began a good work in you will carry it on to completion until the day of Christ Jesus" (Philippians 1 v 6).

In every other area of life we understand sanctification both negatively and positively. To borrow Paul's wording from another part of Ephesians, it is about "putting off" and "putting on". Let's take a simple example we introduced in the last chapter: our speech. As we pursue holiness in speech, we need to honestly evaluate ourselves and do some putting off.

So, "put off falsehood" sits alongside "and speak truthfully to your neighbour" (Ephesians 4 v 25). And "do not let any unwholesome talk come out of your mouths" belongs with "but only what is helpful for building others up according to their needs, that it may benefit those who listen" (Ephesians 4 v 29). We will become more and more godly in speech as we stop doing some things and start doing others. It's Christianity 101.

We think similarly in pretty much every other area of life. Put off. Put on. Repeat.

When it comes to sexual sanctification however, we tend to put nearly all our effort into the *putting off* part of the formula. So we focus on avoiding pornography, or not looking at a woman or man lustfully. We earnestly desire to avoid adultery and perhaps take steps to ensure we do not find ourselves in tempting or compromising situations.

Please hear what we are saying: if this describes you and these are the temptations you are fighting, then praise God for any victories you are enjoying! Sexual sanctification must begin—as every pursuit of holiness does—with putting off. It cannot end there, however. There is also putting on. There is a positive growth in holiness that must be pursued in the bedroom, just as there is in every other area of life.

If sex—as we hope we've shown—is indeed holy in its proper context and yet still marred by the effects of the fall, even in long-married and loving couples, why would we not make it a topic for prayerful progress? What's holding us back? Do we think God isn't interested in what happens on the top floor of our houses? Are we too embarrassed to say grace before we make love, just as we would before a meal? Have we shut God off from one of the most precious gifts that he has given couples?

The answer is almost certainly *yes* to these and other questions.

DEEPER MEANING

This, then, is our case for sexual sanctification—not just the putting off of what we all know we shouldn't be doing, but the putting on also. Our ultimate goal in this is to make sex more meaningful. That doesn't mean simply making intimacy better or more enjoyable. It means pursuing enjoyment and excellence because we know the deeper meaning. It's great to know that meaningful sex and good sex are not enemies of each other. But, as believers in Christ and the church, we must be those who pursue quality because we understand that to which it ultimately points. This is what it means to be *closer*; couples committed to making sex holier.

Expressed this way, perhaps it all sounds a bit alien and even a little uncomfortable, but let us encourage you to stop and think for a moment. Couples already act this way when it comes to the procreative aspect of sex. We're not embarrassed about thinking carefully when a wife might be most fertile in her monthly cycle in order to increase the chances of conception. We might perhaps reflect on what sexual positions are most likely to encourage the little swimmers to reach the egg and boost the opportunities of fertilisation.

In other words, thinking proactively about sex is not an alien concept in some areas. Why should it not be in every area? We've seen that sex is a profound reflection of our union with Christ. In this sense, it is a proclamation. In Bible terms, proclamations happen with both word and symbol: a sermon proclaims Christ; but so does the Lord's Supper. While we shouldn't assume that both have the same cash value in God's economy, we should not want to neglect either. Let's put it this way: if the holy, sexual intimacy a married couple enjoy is a proclamation of a deeper truth, shouldn't you both want it to be clearer? Purer? Better? Isn't sexual sanctification a *good thing*? Don't you want to be *closer*?

QUALITY NOT QUANTITY

Better does not necessarily equal more. As we get older, sexual desires (and capabilities) decrease. You don't have to have been married very long to know this. In his 2020 book, *I Still Do*, experienced pastor Dave Harvey outlines 10 defining moments for long lasting marriages and wisely includes number seven: "When you discover sex changes with age". Better does not equal more; instead, "To run strong, couples have to anticipate changes together and mark them as God's invitation to define normal in a way that suits and serves their particular marriage".

No, better sex means more meaning, deeper intimacy, increased selflessness and greater understanding of your partner. We should not, therefore, build a direct correlation between frequency and excellence. At the same time, however, better sex does not necessarily mean *less*. Christian couples should be finding ways to enjoy one another and increasingly delight in the good gift of intimacy that God has given them, and we should be wary of becoming indifferent to it (so it slips down our priorities and becomes infrequent) or even giving up on sex altogether.

This—believe it or not—is what is happening in the world right now, and it should stand as a warning to those who think most highly about sex: *people are having sex less*. It's surprising because we are constantly bombarded with sex, whether it is the latest box set or the most recent Hollywood blockbuster. But people are, in the real world, actually having less of it.

A September 2018 survey from Mumsnet (the online mums' forum) and its sister site Gransnet (for, you guessed right, grandmas) found that 29% of couples had had sex less than ten times in the last twelve months. That's well below what you might expect based on watching the latest sitcom. In the same survey, 8% of couples had not had sex at all in the last year. Relate—a UK relationships counselling service—conducted a similar survey and found the percentage to be even higher.

We'll discuss what Christians should think of that kind of frequency in the fourth section, where we discover that the most commonly asked question by couples is *How often should we do it?* But for now, the very fact that such statistics make headlines should cause us to stop and think. Quality does not equal quantity—sure. But no sex at all, or very infrequent sex is more likely to reflect a loss of meaning rather than a desire to patiently wait for the ultimate bedroom encounter.

AND NATSAL AGREES

Sex surveys and statistics are notoriously unreliable. Who, after all, wants to reveal intimate details about their behaviour? Lurid headlines often distort or misrepresent the data that is collected. "A man thinks about sex every seven seconds" is a great example of a "fact" that is totally without foundation. But this decrease in people having sex is backed up by more formal research.

Let us introduce you to NATSAL. The National Survey of Sexual Attitudes and Lifestyles is a reputable survey conducted by a top London university (UCL) and the London School of Hygiene and Tropical Medicine. It has been conducted three times, in 1990, 2000 and most recently in 2010, a period which roughly, as it happens, covers the length of our marriage. These surveys are referred to as NATSAL1, NATSAL2 and NATSAL3. There is also an equivalent survey in the USA called the National Survey of Sexual Health and Behavior (NSSHB) conducted by Indiana University School of Public Health.

In broad terms both show similar results and trends. We'll use both surveys in this book, but as neither are from an explicitly Christian perspective, we're going to be careful how we use them. We don't want to describe patterns and behaviours against which believers inevitably start measuring themselves—always a sure-fire way to rob sex of the joy and delight it should bring.

Nevertheless, some trends are useful to reflect on, and perhaps one of the most surprising is that the Mumsnet data is borne out by the more scientific study: people are having surprisingly little sex. What is more, they are having *less* over time. In his book, *Sex by Numbers*, Cambridge statistician Professor Sir David Spiegelhalter helpfully analyses the survey results for us. And here is the number one conclusion: *people are having less sex.* Birds and bees may be doing it. Even educated fleas are doing it, as the song goes. But couples? Not so much.

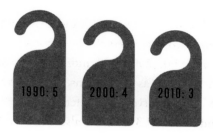

FREQUENCY OF SEX IN THE LAST FOUR WEEKS
SOURCE: NATSAL 1-3, SEX BY NUMBERS

Notice how significant the reduction is. In 1990, sexually active heterosexual adults reported that, in the last four weeks, they had sex (on average) five times. By 2010, this had fallen by 40%, an extraordinary reduction. Christian writer Glynn Harrison, reflecting on these findings in *A Better Story*, says that it is not even as though the perceived quality of the sex has got better. Citing another survey , he shows how a reduction in quantity is not compensated by an increase in quality.

AM I BOTHERED?

Should Christians worry about these findings when it comes to their own lives? At one level the answer is *no*. And let's be honest: statistics can hide a myriad of situations, each couple with their own story to tell. There is however, a deeper truth at stake. It would appear that despite every piece of public propaganda that might persuade us otherwise, people genuinely care less about meaningful sex. They simply, it would seem, can't be bothered. It is too easy to take sexual intimacy for granted and let things slip.

Moreover, the NATSAL3 data shows that in long-standing couples there is also a significant mismatch in sexual desire. This mismatch changes with age, but overall only 63% of men and 59% of women agree that they share a similar level of interest in sex. Perhaps a mismatch is not so surprising to you and borne out in your own experience, but the data suggests that we cannot even take for granted that agreement about sex within our own marriages will be straightforward. This hardly seems to be "holier" sex.

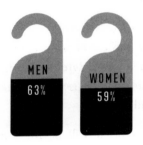

COUPLES WHO SAY DESIRE IS MATCHED
SOURCE: NATSAL 3

GETTING CLOSER

What, then, defines "better" sex? Let us suggest some ways of thinking about this question, depending on your own circumstances.

If sex for you is good, then firstly praise God! Don't take this for granted but commit to making things even better. Sexual sanctification for you is to invest time and energy to take the intimacy you enjoy to new heights of meaning, and to avoid presuming on the good gift that God has given you and the season of joy he has blessed you with. You will be closer to each other, and closer to the pattern that God has set out for you.

If sex is frustrating, then sexual sanctification means believing it *can* be better and working and praying together to see changes which will bring joy to you both. This process may be straightforward and obvious, or it may be difficult and require deep patience. Either way, Christians purposely pursue getting closer. They don't give up.

If sex is difficult, then weep honestly together. Perhaps remember together the closeness you once had, be honest about struggles you currently wrestle with and think and pray together about what small steps you can take to recover your first enthusiasm and joy.

If sex is non-existent (as it will be for some readers), then prayerfully try to work out how you've got to this place and seek the help you need to turn things around.

We've got good news. In each case, God is on your side!

Remember that he thought of sex first, and wants to see us grow in holiness, which means he wants every part of our Christian lives to be sanctified. He wants us to be closer, in every sense. None of this is easy—we don't pretend that it is so and neither should you. It is not—rightly—a subject we are used to talking about. Nevertheless, every Christian couple should be thinking about how to make progress.

WHERE TO START?

All this is hugely daunting, and the first question you may want to ask is *Where do we start?* We want to suggest that the first thing for any Christian couple to do is to see what God has to say. We've already established some broad lessons, but the Bible has more to say about sex than this. We should not be surprised to find that this is so, because God thought of sex from the beginning; he knows the effects sin has on human relationships; and it is his glorious picture of the amazing redemption he has achieved in Christ and the coming consummation of all things. Join us, therefore, as we think about one key passage in the Scriptures and establish some basic principles that will guide us through this complex area.

Knowing these principles is not on its own going to make much of a difference to our marriages: we've got to apply them. And even then, it would be tempting to use them as a kind of first-aid pack or like a defibrillator housed on the outside of a public building. *Need a little jolt in the bedroom?* Then remove pads, select 1000 volts and apply. Such one-off drastic action is not likely to do lasting good.

We want to suggest a better way that will bring you closer. Read about the principles and then use them to talk to one another about the intimacy God has given you. Ask questions of one another. Ask how things could be better; pray about how things could be holier. Keep remembering sex has a deeper significance.

Then in the final section, we've tried to apply the principles to some of the top questions that Christians ask, to help you see how this process works; but it's up to you to make it relevant to your own marriage.

Asking questions is a really good way to make progress in any area of life. Let's go back to our example of speech. As part of "putting off" bad ways, we could ask a friend or spouse, *What do I say that is unhelpful?* Or *What tone of voice do I use that winds you up?* But we should equally be asking, *What could I say that would encourage you?* Or even *What kinds of words do you find most helpful?*

When it comes to sexual intimacy, it's these latter type of questions that we want to help you with. Asking them and answering them honestly and biblically will help you make progress. It should help make sex better. And if you're thinking about sex rightly, that also means making sex purer. It means bringing you closer.

This is the talk that you need to have.

Study and pray. Then apply. It's in this honest talking, praying, giving, trying (and sometimes failing) that God will change you—motives, thoughts and actions, so that sex is not just better, it is holier.

SECTION 2

The principles

Let's be honest: the Bible is not a manual for the bedroom. On the whole this is good news, even though sometimes we would rather have a clearer list of do's and don'ts. What we really need are biblical truths that we can apply to a vastly different and rapidly changing culture. And this is exactly what God's word gives us: timeless principles.

We want to establish five foundational principles from one short passage of the Scriptures, 1 Corinthians 7. The apostle Paul wrote this letter to deal with a church which had lost its way, despite appearing to be in the "super-spiritual" category. All sorts of things were going on which should not have been tolerated, and the letter is Paul's opportunity to re-establish gospel foundations and gospel living in a culture which was extremely worldly. He wanted the Corinthians to pursue sanctification in every area of life. "So whether you eat or drink or whatever you do, do it all for the glory of God" (10 v 31).

In the middle of the letter, Paul responds to a number of questions that the Corinthians have themselves asked, starting right here in chapter 7:

> *Now for the matters you wrote about: "It is good for a man not to have sexual relations with a woman."* [2] *But*

since sexual immorality is occurring, each man should have sexual relations with his own wife, and each woman with her own husband. ³ The husband should fulfil his marital duty to his wife, and likewise the wife to her husband. ⁴ The wife does not have authority over her own body but yields it to her husband. In the same way, the husband does not have authority over his own body but yields it to his wife. ⁵ Do not deprive each other except perhaps by mutual consent and for a time, so that you may devote yourselves to prayer. Then come together again so that Satan will not tempt you because of your lack of self-control. ⁶ I say this as a concession, not as a command. ⁷ I wish that all of you were as I am. But each of you has your own gift from God; one has this gift, another has that.

1 Corinthians 7 v 1-7

We think that there are five key principles in this passage. Together they are a solid set of foundations which will help Christian couples answer most of the questions they have about sexual intimacy and help them pursue holiness, both by putting off and—importantly—putting on. In each case, we will outline and explain the principle, illustrating as we go. Then after we have established all five, we will use them to answer the five most-asked questions about sex that Christians have.

The five principles are these:

1. **Let's do it.** Sex is good, normal and healthy.

2. **Keep taking the tablets.**[*] Sex is a protection against immorality and Satan's temptations.

3. **It's not about you.** Sex is a selfless act which is centred on the other person.

4. **Let's talk about it.** Sex requires communication and openness.

5. **Keep the door closed.** Sex is a private matter for a couple.

Let's dive right in with number one.

---

* *This British phrase is used by medics to urge patients to be consistent in taking the pills (tablets) they have been prescribed.*

PRINCIPLE 1:
LET'S DO IT

We are bombarded with sex. Advertising billboards; box sets; songs on the radio; articles online. You're never more than one click away. Our home internet provider gives us parental protection tools which block inappropriate sites and it never ceases to amaze us how many innocent Google searches are blocked because there's an adult webpage just around the corner.

Perhaps we should not be altogether surprised. The most oft-quoted statistic when it comes to sexual activity is that men think about sex every seven seconds. This dubious measure was dreamt up for a newspaper headline and has since been disproved. However, plenty of studies have been conducted to find out just how often we really do think about sex. The answer, at least according to one US study of psychology students (hardly a representative crowd, to be fair) is 19 times a day for men, 10 times for women. According to statistics expert David Spiegelhalter, that represents just slightly less than we think about food! A little less, but not much.

In fact, today it is more surprising when we come across books, films or music that *don't* contain sexual themes. When tech giant Apple launched its new TV streaming series to compete with Amazon and Netflix one of its unique selling points was that it *wouldn't* feature adult material—a distinction that would have seemed completely unnecessary just a few years earlier.

RESPONDING TO IMMORALITY

In this cultural maelstrom, what are Christians to make of sex? Let's turn to our passage for help. We can't be exactly sure of the problems that gave rise to the questions that the Corinthians had for Paul. Corinth almost certainly contained all the prevailing sexual excesses of the day—everything you would have found in the wider Roman Empire, you would also discover concentrated in this bustling port. If we think we're bombarded, then it's certain that the Corinthians were too.

There are times when this immorality had crept into the church. For example, Paul has already dealt with a case of incest (1 Corinthians 5 v 1), and he has had to show how wrong it is to visit a prostitute (1 Corinthians 6 v 16). However, there were other Corinthian believers who wanted to lift themselves above this worldly thinking and carve out a new path. They believed their super-spirituality meant they were free from such everyday concerns as sexual intimacy. Perhaps this was a way to avoid the temptations of the world; perhaps it was simply a way to show that they had achieved a higher plane.

Either way, they had devised a new motto for married couples and perhaps included it on the church notice sheet: "It is good for a man not to have sexual relations with a woman" (1 Corinthians 7 v 1). *Are they right?* This is the primary question that Paul is responding to.

Everyone else is doing it, they were saying. *It's in your face; it's sinful; it's objectionable; it's evil; let's be different. After all, we're the super-spiritual ones. We're so beyond sex. Let's not do it! That would surely be the spiritual response,* they seemed to believe. In part, at least, it's the same way that some Victorian Christians responded to the gin-alley drunkenness culture of the 19th century, and the saloon culture that led to prohibition in the US in the 1920s. *How can Christians be different and set a better example? We're better than that! By not drinking anything;* that's the answer they came up with.

The Corinthians are not making a point about sex generally. These aren't questions about whether sex outside of marriage is comparable to intimacy within. It is clear from Paul's response that both he and they are thinking of married couples. Instead, they're saying that, since they have the Spirit and since sexual immorality is all around them, it would be a "good" thing if Mr and Mrs Corinthian slept in separate beds.

Perhaps they thought Paul (a single man, remember) might have agreed. However, he could not be clearer about his own view of their sexual temperance movement: *they're just plain wrong.* "But since sexual immorality is occurring, each man should have sexual relations with his own wife, and each woman with her own husband" (v 2).

GOD'S GOOD GIFT TO COUPLES

In other words, sex is a good thing. It needs to be within a marriage for this to be true. That is the point of stating his principle from the point of view of both the husband and the wife in both verse 2 and also in verse 3. Sex outside of this context, by inference, is not good. But the Corinthians should not allow the warped view of sex in the world to deface God's good gift.

In fact, Paul goes even further. Part of the Corinthians' argument is presumably that abstention is good because of the sexual immorality in the world: better to avoid any hint of contamination. Yet Paul argues that it is precisely *because* there is sexual sin that husbands and wives should be giving themselves to one another. The Christians in Corinth do not need to be imagining a higher goal for which to aim: sex is the Creator's plan for marriage. This normality is reinforced in verse 5 where Paul lays down strict guidelines under which a couple may refrain from sex: there has to be "mutual consent"; that it must be only for "a time"; and that it should be for a particular purpose, for prayer. In other words, abstinence is to be the *exception* rather than the *rule*.

Sex, therefore, is a normal, good and holy thing for married couples to do. There isn't a higher level to achieve. God designed sex to be part of healthy, holy marriage. And sex is *unchangeably* healthy for married couples, for what Paul said about Corinth could equally apply to today's culture—"since sexual immorality is occurring".

So our view of sex should not just be that it is normal, good and healthy, it should also be *regular*. "Do not deprive each another", the apostle says (v 5). In 2016, a report in *The Times* newspaper cited a study carried out of over 50s by the Relate counselling service. Of the couples they surveyed, 25% described their marriage as sexless and nearly 3 out of 5 of these were content with that situation. Now there are a myriad of reasons why a couple may not be able to enjoy sexual intimacy, some of them deeply distressing for the couple. Nevertheless, this and other such studies regularly show that the proportion of consciously sexless marriages is growing, and couples are generally happy with that state of affairs.

Christians should *not* be happy with this trend. We have already seen that sex is a good gift from a loving Creator, given for his glory and, like every gift, we do not want to spurn it, neglect it or misuse it. Rather, we want to celebrate and enjoy it, and let it do us the good that God intended. As with any good gift, we must receive it with thanks.

GOOD, AND ALWAYS GOOD

Right at the beginning of time, we see this goodness shine through for Adam and Eve. The one-flesh unit that God created "were both naked, and they felt no shame". The same goodness echoes through the pages of Scripture in, for example, the way that God himself uses beautiful language to describe his own bride, "I looked at you and saw that you were old enough for love, I spread the corner of my garment over you and covered your naked body. I gave you my solemn oath and entered into a covenant with you, declares the Sovereign LORD, and you became mine" (Ezekiel 16 v 8).

We even see this goodness in the depth of intensity captured as the husband and wife sing to one another in Song of Songs. "Let the king bring me into his chambers," sings the bride (Song 1 v 4) and "our bed is verdant" (1 v 16) and "like an apple tree among the trees of the forest is my beloved among the young men. I delight to sit in his shade, and his fruit is sweet to my taste" (2 v 3).

The husband-to-be likewise replies, "Your breasts are like two fawns, like twin fawns of a gazelle that browse among the lilies. Until the day breaks and the shadows flee, I will go to the mountain of myrrh and to the hill of incense" (4 v 5-6). We do not need an encyclopaedic knowledge of Hebrew metaphors to make a guess at what they are saying to one another!

Nevertheless, we also need to be realistic and acknowledge that for some Christians the normality, regularity, goodness and even beauty of sexual relationships is difficult to assent to. There are two reasons for this reluctance. The first is *ignorance*. Many Christians have grown up in families, churches and settings where sex is a taboo subject. Perhaps their parents withdrew them from sex and relationship lessons at school. Perhaps the subject was never mentioned at home. Perhaps all the portrayals they saw on the television or at the cinema were sinful. It's easy, in those understandable circumstances, to develop very negative instincts about sex and to consider it to be a naughty or a bad thing.

Couples where one or both partners have that kind of background need to hear the gentle encouragement of Scripture. Sexual intimacy in its proper context is beautiful: joyful, loving, beneficial—a good gift from a good God. We need to pray that the Spirit would teach us to love his beautiful present as married couples. If you find yourself in this situation, be assured that time is a great healer. What starts off as awkward and nervous can become joyful and beautiful as a couple learn to delight in what God has given them.

BAD EXPERIENCES

The second reason for this reluctance to see sexual intimacy as fundamentally good, is, we believe, because of past *experience*. For some, this may simply be previous sexual experience that we now realise was wrong—for example, a sexual relationship outside of marriage. This is such a common issue that we have written a short appendix (see page 166) for those who find themselves in this situation. More painfully, for others, it may be a past history of sexual abuse. Tragically, it seems such abuse is increasingly common. It can be difficult to disassociate terrible things that have been done to us (or even by us) from the good gift God gives. Again, we have written a short appendix to try to help in these most broken of circumstances (see page 157).

We should let neither ignorance nor experience change the ultimate truth that the Bible asserts—sexual intimacy is a holy gift from a good God It is a thing of beauty, of wonder and of significance to be embraced and enjoyed by married couples.

The wonder of the gift also means, very practically, that it is worth giving our time, energy and emotion—both physical and spiritual—to cultivate the environment in which sexual intimacy can flourish. If sex is indeed good and normal and healthy, then it deserves our best, and any investment we make is going to provide a healthy return. Too often, sexual intimacy in marriage receives the fag-end of our time and the emotional dregs that we can rescue from the busyness of the day. If we really believed in its goodness, then we would reverse this under-investment and celebrate God's good gift to every married couple, with thankfulness in our hearts.

Let's do it.

PRINCIPLE 2:
KEEP TAKING THE TABLETS

Every so often some shocking statistics about Christians and adultery are published. In 2014, for example, the US survey company Barna worked with a Christian purity charity to discover just how many couples faced this issue. They discovered that, among men who self-identified as born-again Christians, 31% admitted to having had an extra-marital affair. The rate was 17% for women. Of those men who had admitted to infidelity, three out of every four had repeated the unfaithfulness with another woman. Adultery, it seems, is a church pandemic.

Even allowing for the breadth of those who describe themselves as "born again" in the USA, these findings are breathtaking. It means that in your small church which includes 20 couples, there may be six or seven where one or other, or both, have been unfaithful. In a large church with 200 couples, it could be ten times that number.

DON'T PRESUME ON FIDELITY

We cannot take for granted that married couples will remain faithful to one another; and the Bible does not take this for granted either. True, there are many reasons why men or women stray sexually. Nevertheless, Paul is very clear that abstention can at least be partly to blame, fanning the flames of a lack of self-control. That is why he is so against the Corinthian approach: "since sexual immorality is occurring..." is how his response begins (v 2).

This same idea is repeated in verse 5 when he is allowing that a short period without sex may be acceptable in order to pray but "then come together again so that Satan will not tempt you because of your lack of self-control". One of the real issues with the Corinthians' self-imposed sexual exile was that couples would simply fulfil their natural God-given sexual urges elsewhere in ungodly ways—and that, argues the apostle, would be countering any good work the Corinthian believers might think they are achieving.

Sex for married couples does many things: it nurtures intimacy; it reinforces our oneness; it is enjoyable; it even helps us sleep! But while it is all of these things, it is not less than a protection against sin. Christian couples need to understand that investing quality time and energy in sex will mean building barriers against sin entering the marriage.

Intimacy is given by God as an antidote to the sexual immorality prevalent in any society. That's expressing the truth quite negatively, so perhaps we can turn it around and state it this way: sex promotes holiness. This is true in general terms because sex is the deepest experience of the significance of marriage, and so it is a regular and profound reminder of what marriage really is. It is also true specifically—to put it bluntly, if you're satisfied at home, you are less likely to go looking for satisfaction elsewhere.

SEX PROTECTS OTHERS TOO

The protection that sex offers is one of the reasons that Paul uses the gift language in verse 7: "I wish that all of you were as I am. But each of you has your own gift from God; one has this gift, another has that." Paul here is segueing into a section on marriage and singleness in general, rather than sex specifically. And both singleness and marriage, he claims, are described using the same Greek word, *charisma*: meaning gifts from God for us to enjoy and use in his service.

Note that these are not gifts to be pursued: they represent objective gifts that we already possess. If we are married, we possess the gift of marriage and we certainly should not be pursuing the gift of singleness! Paul is saying that our status, and all that we enjoy as part of it, is a gracious gift from the great Giver.

Sexual intimacy, as we have seen, is part of the goodness of marriage, and so we need to see that the sexual intimacy married couples enjoy (and, in fact, the sexual abstinence that singles rejoice in) is part of the *charisma* gifting that God gives not only to us, but to all his people. It's important to have this wider perspective: his gifts are given to individuals for the building up of all (a point Paul will make in just a few chapters in 12 v 7).

Therefore, sex is not just a gift to married couples for that particular married couple: it is a gift given to married couples for the whole church. True, in verse 5 of chapter 7, the protection that sex offers does seem to be related to any given husband and wife team: it is their own personal antidote to a lack of self-control. However, Paul's opening counter-argument to the Corinthians is much more general as he describes the prevailing culture—"since sexual immorality is occurring…"

As a married couple enjoy sex they are not simply protecting themselves. They are protecting their immediate family and the church family too. It's obvious when you stop to think about it. Take one example: our observation of pastors who fall sexually is that in nearly every case, the sin is with another member of the congregation. Unsurprisingly, the whole congregation suffers from the fall out.

ADORNING THE GOSPEL

The protection goes wider however. Despite the prevalence of sexual unfaithfulness, infidelity is still seen negatively in the world in general. That may be surprising, and it is true that wandering politicians, for example, no longer immediately resign when they are unmasked. A sexual scandal however, is still front-page news and will still affect their chances of re-election. In our mixed-up world, though people happily watch dramas about adultery and devour scandalous news stories, we *still* disapprove of people who are sexually unfaithful.

And so while Christians who stay faithful adorn the gospel of a faithful God, making it attractive to outsiders, those who stray bring it into disrepute. Adultery risks marriages, families, churches and the very cause of Christ itself.

It is, therefore, not at all negative to say that sex is a protection. And in just the same way we would keep taking our medication for a long-term illness, so when it comes to sex, couples need to maintain the medicine. It's for everyone's good and not just our own.

Speaking this way hardly seems very romantic—it's not something to get the juices of desire flowing. A husband or wife is unlikely to endear themselves to their spouse by saying "I'm making love to you so that you don't go and have sex with anyone else". But protecting our spouses in this way, and thus protecting others is actually one of the most loving things we can do for each other, even if articulating it explicitly is unlikely to make our lover's heart melt.

Sex protects us. It protects others. And in our sinful world, that's something we all need.

Keep on taking the tablets.

PRINCIPLE 3:
IT'S NOT ABOUT YOU

R ead a women's magazine or a men's monthly and you would be forgiven for thinking that good sex is all about what makes *you* feel good. "10 ways to feel great in bed" or "6 steps to better orgasms": articles which seem to direct all our attention towards self-satisfaction. The Christian measure for good sex is altogether different. It is not "was it good for me?" but "was it good for you?" Christian sex is the ultimate act of self-giving, not (as the world might have us believe) the ultimate act of self-expression.

Paul explains this in what—at first glance—might seem rather cold language. He says that "the husband should fulfil his marital duty to his wife, and likewise the wife to her husband" (v 3). Similarly, in verse 4, "the wife does not have authority over her own body but yields it to her husband. In the same way, the husband does not have authority over his own body but yields it to his wife." There is a mutuality about sex which always puts the other person first.

SEXY CHIT CHAT

It is worth considering the language that the apostle uses. "Duty" and "authority" hardly sound like the kind of words that are going to turn anyone on! Some Bible translations are even less seductive—"The husband should give to his wife her conjugal rights" (ESV).

Let's take these phrases one by one. The idea of duty is to pay someone what is owed. Paul uses the same word in Romans 13 v 7 when teaching about paying taxes: "Give to everyone what you owe them: if you owe taxes, pay taxes; if revenue, then revenue; if respect, then respect; if honour, then honour". The latter part of that verse gets some way to describing the concept. Sexual duty is not a cold, reluctant *Oh, if I have to then*. Rather it is a willing giving of what is owed and deserved. It is a way to demonstrate the respect and honour that is due between a husband and a wife.

When we get married, we promise to love and cherish one another. Our sexual intimacy is part of that promise and when a couple give themselves to one another in this way they are doing what they promised to do. In other words, "fulfilling your duty" is nothing less than being faithful, just as God himself is faithful to us. Faithfulness is not simply about what we *don't* do (committing adultery) but what we *do* do: giving ourselves to one another. We cannot claim to be faithful if we do not commit to this.

The language of yielding authority is slightly easier to understand but no less countercultural for that. In our world today, the focus is almost entirely on the authority we believe we have over our own bodies. "It's my own body, I can do what I want with it" is the soundbite that drives all kinds of agendas, perhaps most noticeably the pro-choice abortion lobby. It even drives the sexual agenda, as Christians have recently discovered in the backlash against conservative sexual ethics. The fundamental objection is that "My body is for me—it's nothing to do with you".

In the bedroom, this self-centredness doesn't carry any weight. The husband yields his authority to his wife. He says, in effect, here I am for you; what do you want? Likewise, the wife does the same for her husband, yielding her body up to him. Paul is, we believe, a complementarian when it comes to the issues of men and women: he believes men and women are equally made in God's image but have different roles.

In general terms this means that a husband is to lovingly lead his wife and a wife is to joyfully submit to her husband (see Ephesians 5 v 21-33, for example, or 1 Corinthians 11 v 1-12). Paul says precious little about how this complementary relationship works in marriage in practice—but one surprising area he does cover is sex. The bedroom is to be—it seems— wholly egalitarian! Does this not counter his argument elsewhere? No! For the loving way a husband leads his wife is to yield his body to her authority. And the joyful way a wife submits to her husband is to yield hers to him.

Christian sex is always other-person centred. There is no domination in the bedroom; no hierarchy; no over-ruling; no forcing or coercion; no aggression. Rather, there is mutual submission and always, always, seeking the good of the other. At this point, our view of sex differs sharply from that of the world around us. We believe that *sex is service*. It requires the giving of the whole person to our spouse with nothing held back.

That is one of the reasons why it is the pinnacle of the one-flesh union that the marriage bond creates. Nothing else we do is so other-person centred. This other-person centredness is ultimately what defines good Christian sex. It is not really about quantity or quality (though Christians should not want to skimp on either). It is about giving *all* of yourself to your partner.

YOU FIRST

At this point, there's a very practical issue to address: how do couples stop being a parody of the Laurel and Hardy sketch where both comedians try to get through the door at the same time, getting stuck, then trying again with "After you." "No, after you." "No, after you, I insist" before both getting wedged once more?

The chart shows a survey conducted in 1997 by publisher Random House in the USA as summarised by David Spiegelhalter. It's not particularly scientific but it does reflect nearly every other survey conducted on this topic, both in Europe and the US. Pollsters asked a number of couples what their favoured sexual positions were and mapped the top three variants.

FAVOURED SEXUAL POSITION	MEN	WOMEN
WOMAN ON TOP	45%	33%
MAN ON TOP	25%	48%
FROM BEHIND	25%	15%
OTHER	5%	4%

See how the percentages for preferences as to who goes on top during sex are almost exactly reversed between men and women? If sex is always about putting the other first, how can things ever get going? If the principle were to be strictly applied, lovemaking would descend into a Laurel and Hardy farce—"I'll go on top". "No, I'll go on top" and so on, culminating in both falling onto the floor laughing—the sexual equivalent of Stan and Ollie stuck in the doorway.

We have not included this data to make a point about sexual positions, but rather to show that selflessness could—if misunderstood—lead to absurdity. So what's the answer? Perhaps, you might think, the solution is to take turns: "I decided last time, it's your turn to choose". Perhaps keep a diary to make sure neither misses out? That may be a short-term solution to a highly relational issue, but the real answer is more spiritual and much less calculating.

LEARN TO THINK DIFFERENTLY

The longer-term way to address this issue is to train ourselves to rejoice in differences and learn to delight in what others love rather than our own preferences. We are conditioned by our selfish natures to value what we ourselves love. This is a recipe for disaster in life generally, so we have developed the art of toleration where I can, for the sake of happiness and harmony, put up with what you prefer even if I would rather not.

Such an attitude can easily creep into the bedroom, and does. Let's stick with the example of sexual position. A wife might "put up with" a particular sexual position she does not prefer because her husband does. While this might promote short-term harmony and, on the surface seems very selfless, it is not going to be the foundation for a good long-lasting healthy marriage. It's hardly a union of two minds and bodies.

Instead, the Christian way is to value and delight in the other's opinion and preference. In this particular example, a wife or husband should rejoice that a certain position is bringing a spouse joy. They like it not because *they* like it but because *their spouse* likes it. They like it not *in spite* of their spouse liking it, but *because* their spouse likes it. This is real mutual submission in the bedroom.

Such an attitude is precisely what Paul is describing in Philippians 2 v 1-11. Although he does not have sexual intimacy in view in that passage, the attitude of other-person-centredness applies as much in the bedroom as it does in the rest of Christian life. Our ultimate measure of good sex is therefore determined by asking the question *What is good for you?* Or even *What is good for us?* But never *What is good for me?* That is an important principle to apply to every question we have about sexual intimacy.

It's not about you.

PRINCIPLE 4:
LET'S TALK ABOUT IT

R ead any sexual health manual or agony-aunt column and you cannot help but notice the number of times the solution is to "talk it through". Communication is, of course, key in any relationship, but many couples fail to apply this simple truth in the bedroom.

Suzi Godson is the co-author of *The Sex Book*, a large secular book about intimacy that has been translated into over 15 languages. She is also a regular columnist in the weekend newspapers in the UK. During an interview with *The Irish Times* in May 2017 she said, "It's much easier to have sex than it is to talk about it, but there is a direct and proportional relationship between a couple's ability to communicate honestly, and the level of satisfaction they get from their sexual relationship".

Her views are not simply anecdotal. In a scientific study published in *The Journal of Marital and Family Therapy* in 2017, the authors found a direct correlation between (in women) the number of orgasms and (in both men and women) general levels of sexual satisfaction and the amount of "sexual communication".

Neither Suzi Godson nor the authors of the study have got, as far as we are aware, a particular Christian worldview, yet they are expressing a universal truth which should surprise no-one who believes in a speaking God. God is himself relational—the great Three-in-One—and he speaks to us and delights in us speaking to him. He has made us relational beings who need to speak to each other. Even when we cannot speak (through, for example, physical disability) we always find other ways to communicate. Why should we be surprised that such communication—essential to all relationships—matters behind closed doors also?

INSPIRED SEX TALK

The Song of Songs, the most sexually explicit of all the Bible's 66 books is, essentially, a recorded conversation between a husband and wife. In it we see an inspired and authorised record of their communication—not that every couple's private speech should be so public, but it's helpful for us all to see that communicating about sex is not dirty, wrong or unnecessary but rather vital to the intimacy we crave.

We occasionally run marriage seminars and retreats and ask couples to write down everything they love about being married. They come up with lots of things they delight in, although surprisingly few mention sex (although this may be because we do this exercise early in the seminar and people are a bit wary of mentioning the subject). We then get them to think about what makes any of those characteristics really, really good. For example, couples often cite "friendship" as a key benefit of being married. And what makes friendship really good, we ask? The answer is, of course, *communication*: it is having someone to talk to and with.

Good communication is more than simply offering up our opinions. It is about relationship and so it is also about listening; sharing both likes and dislikes, joys and difficulties, being honest and responding lovingly and so on. Bedroom communication follows the same pattern.

We're with Suzi Godson on this. If you cannot communicate, it is highly unlikely that you can have good sex. Or, to express it more positively, if you want to enjoy and delight in really good sexual intimacy, you have to be working on good communication. The two always go together. The first response to couples who struggle in this area is always, "Have you talked about it?"

We can see this principle in our passage in 1 Corinthians, even though it is perhaps not as explicit as the other lessons we have learned so far. How does a husband know how to yield his body to his wife (v 4)? How does a wife know how to do the same? How does a couple know what a "time" is in verse 5? Some may find it frustrating that Paul does not set out more precise boundaries. Wouldn't it have been more useful for him to tell couples not to absent themselves from sex for, say, more than a week. Why is he so vague? In part, as we shall see in a moment, this is because sex is a private matter. However, it is also because all through the passage Paul assumes that a husband and wife will be talking about these matters.

Nothing is assumed or taken for granted when it comes to sex. For example, we cannot presume to know exactly what our partner likes as preferences—likes and dislikes change over time. We cannot conclude that we have our spouse completely worked out. We're never going to be able to work through these issues unless we communicate.

None of this should surprise us. We don't need to do much of a Bible survey to see that words are a key theme in Scripture. For as Christians, we were given new birth "through the word of truth" (James 1 v 18); Jesus himself sustains all things "by his powerful word" (Hebrews 1 v 3); and the growth of the church itself happens as the members of the church speak "the truth in love" (Ephesians 4 v 15). Why would this not apply to one of the most important aspects of married life?

WHEN IT'S NOT SO EASY

Some couples find this a very hard battleground. Talking things through can be difficult anyway, but when it comes to something so personal, it's even harder. Being able to say, "I really don't like that" or "Could you…" can be a very difficult thing for some people to do. The awkwardness of this kind of communication is borne out by one question asked by the NATSAL organisers. They asked couples whether they found it easy to talk about sex to their partner. The results are surprising.

EASY TO TALK TO A PARTNER ABOUT SEX?	MEN	WOMEN
AGE 16-44	36%	26%
AGE 16-74	31%	25%

NATSAL3 TABLE 78

In our minds, at least, these percentages are shockingly low. Across all ages (16-74), only one quarter of women in relationships felt that they could easily talk to their partners about sex. Only a few more men felt it was a straightforward thing to do. There is no direct statistical correlation between this data and overall sexual satisfaction. Nevertheless, it is noticeable that the level of those who are very content with their sex lives is just 22% for men and 23% for women (NATSAL table 73). No wonder therapists are always asking, "Have you talked about it?"

To be clear, we're not thinking here about talking *during* sex. That subject belongs in a different category. Some couples like to do this—some prefer silence. Some like whispers. Others like more noise. That's more to do with being selfless and learning what pleases the other person and serving them in this way. The Bible, in fact, has nothing to say about this kind of communication, one way or the other. Instead, when it comes to communicating, it seems the Bible has two main topics that we need to consider.

SEX TALK

First, the Bible encourages us to use speech to *anticipate* sex and cultivate intimacy. Although these kinds of words do not feature in 1 Corinthians, it seems—especially in Song of Songs—that communication makes a big difference in getting us ready for good sex and nurturing the relationship in which it takes place.

Most of the eight chapters of this poetic book work in this way—they are heightening expectation, longing, fondness and love between a couple so that the moment of consummation is deep, meaningful and full of joy. Sex, strictly speaking, does not *need* this kind of verbal foreplay to be good. It can be immediate and urgent. But, on the whole, God's pattern is that sexual intimacy is a reflection of a deeper bond that is enhanced by good, holy, private talk.

Second, we need to talk *about* sex to one another, husband and wife. Therapists sometimes call this kitchen-table sex talk. The kitchen table, for most people anyway, is one of the least sexy parts of the house. Sitting there (we're assuming it's just the two of you) surrounded by the dirty plates and leftover food is the perfect place to think about sex in a dispassionate way. It is not that sex is itself passion-less, but sometimes we need to talk about it in an objective way when we know it won't lead anywhere.

We need to be able to evaluate our intimate lives at times other than when we're catching our breath. It's easier to answer honestly, "How is it for you at the moment?" in those "kitchen-table" moments than when you're recovering from an orgasm. Paul assumes in his passage that this kind of communication is always going on. That's going to be how we come to conclusions about really important questions like "How do I yield myself to you?" (v 4). It's going to be the best place to tackle sin, perhaps unhelpful thoughts we're struggling with, or anxieties that are making sex difficult.

Both these forms of communication, like all Christian talking, require openness. The phrase Paul uses in Ephesians 4 cannot be bettered—we are to speak "the truth in love". According to that chapter, this is how the church is built; and it is how healthy marriages are developed also. And given the centrality of intimacy to marriage, such discussion needs to take place.

We're not here to tell you how best to heighten the anticipation of sex. You need to work out your own foreplay without our assistance. We do, however, want to encourage you to have more of those kitchen-table chats. They're essential to tackling problems and cultivating joys, and surprisingly few Christian couples invest quality time in these kinds of discussions.

There are obvious reasons for this. Two UK-based researchers working for the National Health Service discovered in 1999 that the main reason that couples did not communicate about sex was fear of a negative reaction. Each partner was worried what the other might think. Such concern is completely understandable.

But, for Christians, the gospel of Christ where all are counted equal (Galatians 3 v 28) allows us to be honest with each other and not fear loving critique. Our identity comes from knowing who we are in Christ, not from what others—even those close to us—think of us.

It should be the case, therefore, that when it comes to talking about anything, Christians should be much better at it. And for committed married couples, that must mean *let's talk about it*.

PRINCIPLE 5:
KEEP THE DOOR CLOSED

In 2007, as part of a European-wide study into premature ejaculation, a group of urology researchers conducted some interesting research. They asked couples in five countries to have sex twice in a week in the way they normally would. As part of the research they asked each couple to estimate what they called the IELT—a technical term meaning the "intravaginal ejaculatory latency time": what you and we would call the time it takes for a man to come once penetration has begun; to put it bluntly—how long does he last?

They were then asked to measure the real IELT, and the study compared the estimates to the actual findings. Although using a stopwatch hardly sounds like a sexy way to spend an evening, the study has proved to be important for the treatment of sexual health problems. Along the way, however, it reveals something very interesting about sex in general.

In each of the five countries, couples estimated that sex measured in this way would last between 10 and 12 minutes (except the Italian respondents who estimated it would last 16 minutes: draw your own conclusions). When they came to measure the actual duration, the average was the same for every country: 10 minutes—even in Italy.

Why are these interesting results? It is because they show—on a very simple measure—that there's not a lot of difference between us. Men and women worry far too much about what others are doing (or not) or what physiology they have, instead of concentrating on themselves as a couple. As we shall see in the next section, this is at the root of most of the questions couples have about sex—am I doing it right?—for which the measure is too often—what are others doing?

This is true in other areas. Following up on the perennial question that men (rather than couples) ask, TV Doctor Mark Porter summarised several surveys in typically candid fashion: "Does size matter? Most women say not, and if anything a few prefer their partners' penises to be smaller." Not only do we therefore have permission to ignore every junk email promising enlargement, we can also see the absurdity of comparisons.

In the next section, we'll consider some other questions couples ask and we'll discover that the reason they ask them is that they think everyone else has it better. This is not the Christian way.

JUST THE TWO OF YOU

The Christian principle is this: *sex is private.* That might seem like an obvious statement when it comes to the sexual act itself but it's a concept that's always under fire. For many couples, of course, the challenge is keeping it private—especially from house-wandering or sleep-walking children (we recommend a lock on the bedroom door). Perhaps for others, there is the alluring enticement of it being more public. Do you find the idea of making love outdoors exhilarating? If you do, let us offer a gentle warning: you are running the risk of being arrested for indecent exposure.

Our principle, however, is not about avoiding nosy toddlers or rolling in the long grass. It is broader: your own sex life is private to you as a couple. Except in a few circumstances— we'll talk about these in a moment—you should not be discussing your bedroom life with others, even your closest friends. You need to keep both the metaphorical as well as the physical door well and truly shut.

We can see that from our key passage. As we've seen, Paul is responding to a particular question about whether, in a sexually charged and corrupted world, celibacy is a good thing. His answer is straightforward: *No!* In fact, couples should be enjoying appropriately regular sex. His answer, naturally, begs another question in our minds—"how often is that?" Paul seems to leave things hanging. What is "a time" in verse 5? A week? A month? A year?

You may find Paul's vagueness frustrating. Why couldn't he be more specific? If you want a more specific answer, don't worry, we'll have a go at helping you answer the question for yourselves later. For now, however, we need to see a more general point: *Paul doesn't give an answer at all.* He is happy to leave the answer to the couple. The principle is established, regular sexual intimacy and no celibacy, but precisely what this means is left up to the couple to work out. It is not left—notice—to the wife's brunch girlfriends or the husband's buddies at the bar. It is for the couple themselves to determine the answer between them.

GOOD FOR SOCIETY; PRIVATE TO YOU

Sex is a good thing—as we have already seen. It is to be celebrated and cherished in couples, in the church and—in its proper place—in society itself. Yet despite its public good, it is a purely private thing. The husband and wife are a one-flesh team (spiritually and physically) and Paul wants married couples to work together to think these matters through.

Why does it matter? It matters for two key reasons. First, our primary accountability when it comes to sexual enjoyment is not our friends, glossy magazines or even helpful books on sex. It is our partner—the one that God has given to us to be our life-long companion. When we start discussing our sex lives with others, we break this bond of intimacy and dependency that God himself has created.

Second, we are always under pressure—whether we realise it or not—to conform. In a world where we are bombarded with sexual stories and statistics we can find ourselves under great pressure to listen to other voices rather than the one that matters most: the husband or wife we are serving in our marriage. We've quoted these statistics, therefore, not to give you a comparative measure, but to encourage you to see just how normal you probably are. For the most part, you don't need to be worrying about others and what they do.

A NEW NORMAL?

The real danger comes not from data surveys which only geeks like us read. No, the real danger is much closer to home. Imagine two couples, Bob and Belinda and Steve and Sue. One day Bob is chatting to his mate, Steve, and Steve says to him—in an unguarded moment —"Sex is so great at the moment: Sue comes every time we make love, it's fantastic". Not only is that a breach of a confidence, what's it going to do to the first couple? It's going to establish an expectation for them (or, at least, for Bob) for what "normal" sex should be like—which is not "normal" at all.

In fact, Bob and Belinda may be very happy with their current sex life but the moment of hearing something that is inherently private will undermine their own intimacy and possibly even drive a wedge between them as a couple. Bob is going to go home and worry that his wife is not so orgasmic. Maybe it's his fault? Maybe it's hers? But if Steve and Sue can do it, there must be something wrong if they cannot.

If the couple themselves are unhappy then of course they must talk about it and work things out: they must establish their own "normal". But by opening the bedroom door, the well-intentioned friend has broken the principle, ended up undermining another God-given marriage and almost certainly broken his wife's confidence into the bargain.

Similarly, imagine that Sue herself is out shopping with Belinda, Bob's wife. They are in the health aisle of the supermarket and Sue reaches out for some lubrication, saying to Belinda, "I need this because it makes having sex every day more enjoyable". Again, not only is a confidence broken, but Belinda—who is happy with her once a week swinging-from-the-chandeliers date night with Bob—now worries that she's not really serving her husband who she might think wants a lot more sex than he is getting.

These stories are somewhat superficial, but in each case it is the privacy of sex which has been broken and relationships damaged as a result. In general, Christians are better at maintaining appropriate secrecy than others. We don't—for example—tend to go out and drink to a level where intimate secrets pour out. But we must not take it for granted that this is the case, and we must be especially careful not to establish a false "normal" for other couples.

PRIVATE FOR US TOO—MOSTLY

You will have noticed so far that we have not really talked about ourselves at all as some Christian books about sex are prone to do. Neither are we about to. When we begin to help you apply these principles to some of the most often asked questions, we are going to try to do so dispassionately and will certainly not be telling you what *our* answers are. It is literally *none of your business!* In fact, knowing how we've addressed these issues between ourselves will not actually help you work things out for yourselves, because we are not your measure. You are a one-flesh unit created by God. You are chosen by the Lord for one another. You and your relationship is unique. Therefore you are your own measure.

There are a couple of exceptions to this general rule. First, sometimes couples need help. Things are so difficult, painful or awkward that the only solution is to talk them through with someone else and seek pastoral or professional assistance. Our view is that this is always best done (initially, at least) together. Don't seek help unilaterally. Getting help for difficult times is one of the reasons God has put us in local churches. Even though this may be the most awkward topic of discussion, in your church you will often find older couples who can advise, guide and pray through tougher seasons.

Second, when there is abuse in a marriage it needs to be dealt with right away. Abuse—emotional, sexual or physical—is *always* wrong and an abuser must not be able to claim the right to privacy to prevent someone who is being abused from reporting it to the appropriate authorities. Getting help can be an important step to dealing with this. But on the whole, sex is private and should stay that way.

This privacy principle does not, of course, contradict our previous assertion that sex requires communication. Sex is private to you *as a couple*, but not to you *as individuals*. Do not keep things hidden from each other. That will not enhance lovemaking. Ultimately, it will undermine it. To extend the metaphor, you should make love with the lights on but the bedroom door closed: no one else is allowed in, but there should be total illumination between the two of you.

Keep the door closed.

BRINGING IT
ALL TOGETHER

We've now established five foundational biblical principles, each derived from our one passage in 1 Corinthians. Many people think the Bible does not really answer our specific questions about sex, but the truth is that it gives us something far better. God gives us a framework to answer all the questions raised by our constantly changing world and lifestyles.

We have not written this book with a view to simply making your sex life better (though we hope it will). Our aims are higher. Every Christian couple should be hoping and praying for sex to be sanctified—more holy. Every husband and wife team should be longing to be closer. That means, we believe, for sex to be more meaningful to us as couples, helping us to experience the intimacy, selflessness and oneness that Christ and his bride enjoy.

The good news is that this goal is not inconsistent with sex being better. Not at all. More meaningful is always better.

But it is important to see—as we delve into questions—that *sanctification* and not *performance* is always our ultimate goal; *closeness* rather than individual fulfillment. So, with this in mind, let's learn how to apply the goodness, protection, selflessness, communication and privacy of sex to the particular circumstances we face.

SECTION 3

The questions

M ost couples have questions about sex. There's nothing unusual nor abnormal about this. When two people join together in marriage, they're bringing with them a whole heap of stuff—emotional, theological, physical—from their previous lives. Suddenly they're thrown together and told to make it work. The challenges don't stop there.

Life changes us. Sometimes those changes are gradual. We hardly notice that we are getting older, and our capabilities change with us. Sometimes those changes are more significant—a serious illness for example, or the birth of a child. Both types of change mean we have to be constantly readapting our lives to reflect the God-ordained circumstances we find ourselves in.

Most couples do a pretty good job of making the constant micro-adjustments to life that such changes require. We also make a reasonable attempt at coping with the macro-events that make immediate (and not always expected) change just as necessary. Such change affects every area of life, including sexual intimacy. And this is why most—if not all—couples have questions about sex. In general, couples have a stab at answering these for themselves: they work things out in the bedroom as they do in every other part of marriage.

We want to go further, however, and show you how to apply the Bible's principles to answer the particular questions you may have, rather than, say, tossing a coin. We want you to tackle the questions you have, rather than just ignore them. As we shall see, and you may yourselves have already discovered, unless you work at creating time for quality sex, it is easy to lose your way. This is too important a subject to neglect or put in the procrastination pile as just something else that will get sorted out tomorrow.

Moreover, we want to make sure you are answering your questions with the principles that God so graciously gives. There's nothing inherently wrong with, for example, sexual counselling or assistance from your family doctor. Indeed, seeking such help may be a very important and necessary step for you. But we must set all the counsel we receive in the context of the foundational principles that God himself establishes in his word.

Most of all, we want sex to be sanctified and increasingly so. We want the intimacy we enjoy to be a meaningful reflection of the depths of the oneness the church shares with Christ Jesus. And that means the pursuit of physical, emotional and spiritual betterment. This is *closer*.

THE TOP-TEN COUNTDOWN

Every now and again, surveys ask people (both those who are Christians and a more mixed group) their top ten questions about the practicalities of sexual intimacy. We're not surprised that, over time, the answers to these surveys are nearly always the same. There are, of course, one or two minor differences, and Christians tend to ask slightly different questions from those who think of sex in a more worldly way. Only one of the questions we shall try to help you answer (number four for the curious) has entered into these lists in the last ten years.

You may recognise some of your own questions in this list. The top-ten countdown for Christians goes something like this:

1. How often should we make love?
2. Should a woman have an orgasm every time?
3. Is it ok for Christians to have oral sex?
4. Is it ok for Christians to have anal sex?
5. What should we think about sex aids?
6. Is masturbation wrong?
7. What sexual positions are acceptable for Christians?
8. What do we do about mismatched desire?
9. How do I find my wife's G-spot?
10. What language/words should we use in private?

Christians have other questions too. Some of the other issues we face are deeply difficult and traumatising—for example, what to do when a husband is hooked on porn or how to recover intimacy after an affair. Those are real questions, but outside the remit of this book. There are a number of good resources that will help you in these areas; but you can still apply each of the principles to each of the issues.

Nor are we going to answer all of the top ten. We have deliberately restricted ourselves to the top five for two reasons. First, the top five change very infrequently. They are a pretty common set of questions, while numbers six through ten vary a bit more. Second, we hope that by showing you how to answer each of these questions using the Bible principles we have established, you will have a way of answering any other questions you might have.

That's right—*any*. We have confidence that the Bible's principles are good and sufficient. So, by equipping you to answer five, we're trusting that we're equipping you to answer not just ten, but as many as you have. You will also discover along the way that many of the questions are connected. So, without wanting to spoil the surprise, husbands will stop hunting for their wife's G-spot (Q9) when they learn in our explanation of question 2 that it probably doesn't exist anyway. Questions about frequency (Q1) and mismatched desire (Q8) are closely connected. But let's not get ahead of ourselves.

Q1: NOT TONIGHT, DARLING

HOW OFTEN SHOULD WE MAKE LOVE?

In 2008, *The Denver Post* feature writer Douglas Brown and his wife Annie made an extraordinary commitment to one another. Brown had just returned from attending a conference about sex addiction, and had been struck by one European presenter who had talked about the proliferation of "hundred-day clubs"—groups of men who had not had sex with their wives for 100 days. Once the children had gone to bed and he had settled back into his favourite chair, he repeated the shock statistics to his wife, who was unsurprised. She'd heard it all on Oprah, she said. There and then they made their crazy commitment. Why don't we promise, they said, to make love to one another every single day for 101 days. Let's create, in effect, a better kind of hundred-day club. Plus one.

Their book *Just Do It: How One Couple Turned Off the TV and Turned on Their Sex Lives for 101 days (No Excuses!)* describes how they reached their goal and the fun they had along the way. It quickly became an international bestseller. It's not a Christian book, nor is it entirely wholesome as it breaks just about all of our five principles at one point or another. Nevertheless, their odyssey reveals two important truths that will not surprise you if you've read this far. First, you have to work at finding time for sexual intimacy. It's easy to fall into membership of the original hundred-day club with practically no effort whatsoever. And second, both Doug and Annie testify to the effect that the successful experiment had on their marriage. They felt stronger together, closer and more intimately connected—and not just in the bedroom. They felt, they said, like a team. We might even call that "one-fleshness".

We're not suggesting this is the answer for you. It may be. Or it may not. But it does reveal that the question "How often" should not be too readily dismissed.

FREQUENCY MATTERS

This is what we need to understand—because sex matters, frequency matters. The question, "how often" is therefore a good question for couples to be working through. We've already seen back in chapter 3 that as many as 25% of marriages might be considered sexless—that is, intimacy is either non-existent or so infrequent that it hardly seems to count at all.

There are many reasons why Christian couples also fall into this barren pattern. For some, their experience of sex is just not that good. And if something fails to get your heart racing, why bother? I (*Adrian*) don't particularly like Marmite (a uniquely British delicacy), though I don't actively hate it. And, given a choice, why would I bother? I (*Celia*) feel the same about honey. Our family picnics, therefore, rarely feature either.

For other couples, sex comes associated with guilt. Everybody is doing it, and the world seems to enjoy it, on the whole. Can it really be right for Christians to also enjoy something that the world enjoys so much? Let's not get carried away, they think. Let's put a brake on and take a different path.

Many husbands and wives simply seem to have mismatched desires and so find it very difficult to work out a strategy for sexual frequency that works for both of them. Others find that making time for sex in their season of life is just too difficult.

All these are real pressures. They therefore require us to have real answers. This is especially important because very few people seem to want *less* sex. Buried deep in the NATSAL survey is a set of subjective questions about quality and frequency of sex—how good it was, and how often it was.

The table sets out the responses to the question on frequency; they are very illuminating. Across both sexes, hardly anyone wanted less sex. Just under half were happy with things as they were, with the remainder (52%) wanting sex "a bit more often" or "much more often". The proportion was slightly higher among men than women, but not wildly so.

PREFERENCE FOR FREQUENCY OF SEX	MALE	FEMALE
MUCH MORE OFTEN	18%	13%
A BIT MORE OFTEN	43%	34%
ABOUT RIGHT	38%	49%
A BIT LESS OFTEN	1%	3%
A LOT LESS OFTEN	0%	1%

NATSAL3 TABLE 77

There's a reasonable chance therefore, that whatever pattern you have settled into is not quite doing it for either of you or both of you. So, let's apply our five principles and see why this matters and how we can go about coming up with a better answer.

LET'S DO IT

Paul's response to the Corinthians, remember, is that sex is good, healthy and normal and therefore couples—except in very specific circumstances and even then for only a short while—should not be giving up on it. We expect that very few readers will be thinking precisely the way the Corinthians were thinking. Super-spiritual Christianity of this kind doesn't seem to be all the rage right now. Nevertheless, the practical result might very well be the same. Sex has been relegated in importance and neglected as a result. In the wider world this is borne out by the statistics we saw right at the beginning of the book where we discovered that sexual frequency has taken a significant downturn over the last three decades.

Moreover, Christians should want to have sex *not just for the physical and emotional high it gives us,* but because we understand that it is a gift given to us as couples for our good. We carve out time for other activities that benefit us: whether it is a daily devotion or a weekly run. Why would we not do likewise for sex?

So, the first answer to questions about frequency is to ensure that both husband and wife see the need to enjoy intimate moments together. In her book *365 Nights,* Charla Muller describes how she embarked on an experiment that makes Doug and Annie whom we met at the beginning of the chapter seem like rank amateurs. For her husband's 40th birthday, she offered him sex every day for a whole year. To his credit, he initially refused the gift (a reaction we'll return to in just a moment). However, she made the offer because she understood that intimacy was draining away from their marriage and they needed to be intentional about maintaining it.

Our first principle allows us to see that this is a subject that we are right to take seriously and be intentional about. Such intentionality is not unromantic—quite the opposite. And it is precisely because we, as Christians, understand the goodness of sex that we take this view. Christians should also keep remembering that sex is the best and most intimate (though not the only) expression of the one-flesh union that is marriage. In a very few cases it is ok for marriages to be sexless (for example when a physical illness prevents intimacy), but for most of us we need to understand that a marriage without sex runs the real risk of not being a marriage at all.

Stephen Snyder, a secular psychologist, recognises this truth: "Sex is 20 per cent of a marriage when it's going well, but 90 per cent when it's not", he said in a recent press interview. Moreover, psychologists recognise something called the Westermarck effect (named after a Finnish anthropologist): a sexless marriage essentially becomes like a relationship between a brother and a sister. What's so wrong with that, you may wonder? The wrongness is precisely because a husband and wife are *not* a brother and sister. They are a one-flesh unit, created by God. Brothers and sisters don't sleep together; husbands and wives do.

So, how does this principle affect you? At the very least, it should show itself in a joint commitment to make sure sexual intimacy is not neglected: it should be a priority for you both, whatever season of life you find yourselves in. Just like all of God's good gifts, it is to be received with thanksgiving (1 Timothy 4 v 4).

KEEP TAKING THE TABLETS

If sex in your marriage is to guard against immorality, then the answer to the question "How often?" needs to be "at least as often as needed to protect us and others". In chapter 3, when we established this principle, we highlighted that thinking this way about sex hardly seemed very romantic. Planning sex with our spouse so that no one else will seems remarkably *un*romantic. However, we want to suggest to you that it's not cold at all if it's God's means of protection. When we ask our car passengers to make sure they're buckled in, we're not acting as killjoys to make their journey as miserable as possible. We're doing it because we love them and we want them to be protected should anything happen on our journey.

In fact, it's an extraordinary grace that we can protect one another in this way. There is sexual temptation wherever you turn: on every TV; on every bookcase; in every internet search. If either of us could protect the other from that evil, why would we avoid doing so?

Earlier we showed how the frequency with which couples enjoy sex is declining rapidly and we hinted at the fact that there are some obvious reasons for it. Here's the chief one: couples are having less sex together, *but more sex on their own.*

The chart shows the data for men and women across different age groups who responded positively to the question "Have you masturbated in the last four weeks?" Sadly, there is no like-for-like data from the previous two surveys as the question was only asked of the first age group (16-24) in 1990 and not at all in 1980, probably reflecting a belief that once you were in a committed relationship there was no need to seek satisfaction on your own.

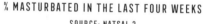

% MASTURBATED IN THE LAST FOUR WEEKS

SOURCE: NATSAL 3

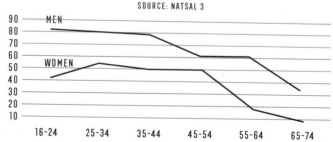

No doubt some of these responses (very high for men, reasonably high for women) reflect the easy access to and use of pornography. But even so, there must be a deeper issue at stake which drives men and women to have solo sex rather than meaningful couples-sex. The answer is almost certainly that it is easier. Such behaviour avoids commitment and does not require the selfless humility that we have seen characterises Christian sex.

Immediately, we can see, from a Christian context, the protective value of sex breaking down. There's no reason to suspect that the data is particularly different for believers. If a Christian husband or wife is masturbating regularly on their own, they are almost certainly using porn to do so. They are probably entertaining fantasies of being with other men or women, which the Bible calls adultery. There is no protection from adultery in masturbation.

Of course, it would be wrong for someone to immediately blame their partner for such behaviour: individuals have to take responsibility for their own actions. At the extreme, the husband who sleeps with another woman cannot point the finger at his wife and say, "It's your fault". But a couple who fail to maintain their sexual intimacy should not be surprised when the protection it offers disappears.

IT'S NOT ABOUT YOU

Remember Charla Muller with her 40th-birthday gift to her husband? He's called Brad, by the way, and he deserves a medal because when she offered him this extraordinary present he first of all fell off his chair—and then turned her down. Charla records in her book how she was indignant at his reaction. *Didn't he want to have sex with her every day for a year?* Brad—and we like this guy more and more—explains how of course he wants to; he's a hot-blooded male. But he's concerned that *she* doesn't really want to. She's only doing it for him, and he wants to please her. He's right of course, and they talk it out and work it through. Her book's title, *365 Nights*, gives an indication of how this all unfolded.

Their story is interesting. Just spend a moment thinking about the planning, the scheduling, the talking-to-yourself that was required to make this offer a reality. They had young kids at the time, so it wasn't straightforward. They had demanding lives. Charla freely admits that they had days when she didn't fancy sex, and others when Brad didn't. But, she says, the discipline of the offer made them realise that it was not all about what they wanted as individuals but how they could give themselves to one another.

We're not, for one moment, suggesting that you take a similar approach (though Charla's unscientific conclusion to her year-long project is to suggest to other couples that their own "magic number" for frequency of sex is "twice whatever you're doing now"). Nor are we suggesting that setting yourself unrealistic goals is necessarily a good thing. Yet in some strange way their story reflects our biblical principle. Good sex is about our spouses, not about us. And that means we can't answer the frequency question without understanding how often our partner would like to cuddle up on the couch.

GETTING THROUGH THE DOOR

Back in chapter 3, we used the rather absurd illustration of Laurel and Hardy trying to squeeze through a door, but the reality is that the frequency question is a little more complicated than that. Both Stan and Ollie *wanted* to get through the door. The question was not desire, it was just whose desire came first.

In many marriages, there is not always matched desire. To push the illustration a little further, we don't always want to both go through the door; some of us are quite happy staying where we are, thank you very much. The NATSAL researchers explored this question and asked couples about mismatched desire (they tested what they termed "similar levels of sexual interest"). The data are almost identical for men and women. A healthy 60% report matched desire (though older couples report higher levels than younger couples). But 25% report a marked mismatch, a potential for disagreement, especially when it comes to issues of frequency. There is, however, virtually no difference between men and women at any particular age point, rather disproving the theory that sexual appetite falls away in different sexes at very different rates.

This principle, remember, is not simply about understanding your spouse's needs and putting up with them. That may be a way to address some practical issues in marriage, but it sure is going to be hard work when it comes to sex. Let's imagine you want a bit more sex and your husband or wife goes along with it, a little reluctantly, because they want to be faithful and apply this principle. That's hardly a turn on, is it? It may be a short-term solution, but it's not the long-term key to happiness.

No, as we suggested earlier in the book, applying this principle is ultimately about learning to enjoy what your partner likes. So, to use an imaginary and somewhat arbitrary example, if you're a once-a-week guy married to a once-a-day gal, you've got to learn to love what your partner loves which—in this rather trite example—is going to be stretching for both of you because there's a world of difference between "1 in 7" and "7 in 7". Yet, ultimately, it is this attitude which will bear true and lasting fruit in your marriage.

There are many ways you could sense whether there is something to work through in this area. For example, if one of you is always snuggling and fondling, there's a pretty good chance they are hoping it might go somewhere. You can read the signs, we're sure. But there is no avoiding that the only real way to answer the question of frequency is to apply our fourth principle.

LET'S TALK ABOUT IT

Perhaps without realising it, Charla and Brad have given us a supreme example of communication. They talked it through. They realised that the commitment they were taking on required more than just a "good idea, bud?" kind of conversation. It required thoughtfulness. It required planning. It required managing work commitments. It required baby-sitters. It even, on one occasion, required a warm blanket (you'll have to read the book). None of this could have happened without communication.

Couples are never going to be able to answer the question "How often" unless they talk openly and honestly about it. And that includes conversations that go beyond "tonight, love?" to ones that deal with practical issues such as creating both the time and environment. It includes very personal but real issues, for example, what intimacy looks like for you during a wife's monthly period or the development of some radical solutions and commitments, particularly if both of you are tired all of the time.

Yet without a commitment to communication, none of these conversations will happen. Remember that good communication is not simply about talking. It also includes non-judgmental listening. That can be tough, particularly if you have not grappled with the fourth principle of selflessness. Many conversations between couples are veiled or coded methods for trying to get your own way.

Imagine our couple who have mismatched desires. It would be easy for the once-a-day woman to have a conversation with her husband which has as its objective getting her reluctant partner as near to her target as possible. That's not *communication*; that's *negotiation*. And sex is not a commodity nor is a marriage a business partnership. So good communication needs both the honesty and humility that characterise every good Christian relationship and must be exemplified in marriage.

KEEP THE DOOR CLOSED

Finally, we've got to remember that the answer to your question is private to you. Even if we were willing (which we're not), there's absolutely no point us telling you our conclusion to this question. Both Doug and Annie Brown, and Charla and Brad Muller have not necessarily helped us here. We have used their stories because they helpfully illustrate some of the points we have been trying to make. But they are their own couples. They've chosen to share their privacy for journalistic reasons. In some ways that's helpful to us.

But don't think they set your standard. Only you set your measure. There are some boundaries, of course. Paul sets one in 1 Corinthians 7. Abstention is not a valid answer—or, at least, only for "a time" which implies that some regularity is desirable. If you want to press us as to what that means, our go-to sex expert Suzi Godson reports on several surveys which suggest that happiness and contentment increase proportionally with frequency to four times a month (once a week), but then increased sexual frequency makes little difference to well-being. Perhaps that once a week target *is* a starting point?

But really. It's down to you. It's your decision and one for you to be happy with yourselves and keep to yourselves. Your friends, neighbours, or books are not your measure. You are.

CRUNCHING THE NUMBERS

What does all this add up to? The chances are, the answer to the question "How often?" for you as a couple is not going to be "a bit less". It would be surprising to us if you were different from almost entirely every other couple in the world. If you're anything like average then you've got it about right already or need to enjoy intimacy more than you do. However, there is no way for us to answer this question for you, other than help you apply these principles. Sex is good and does you good. It protects you and your spouse, and others too. So it's worth serving your partner, and talking about how you might do so.

Who knows? Perhaps Charla is right and the answer to the question "How often?" really is "twice as much as right now". But it's your question and therefore, with God's help, your answer too.

Being *closer* means talking to one another and finding your happy place where intimacy can and does signify all that God intended it to be for you, as often as you like.

Q2: THE BIG O

SHOULD A WOMAN HAVE AN ORGASM EVERY TIME?

Take a deep breath and let's talk about a subject that leaves most people breathless—the female orgasm. Unsurprisingly, the question of whether women should have an orgasm every time they enjoy sex with their husband is near or at the top of most people's lists. And it's not just a question for wives to think through. For sure, it's a common enough topic for women—spurred on by the portrayal of sex in the media and the relentless push to achieve "better" orgasms from the glossy mags.

It's also, however, a question men ask. *A lot.*

But they don't always vocalise it, perhaps because it's difficult for a man to understand sexual intimacy outside of his own experience—which is virtually *all* about orgasm. Estimates vary, but approximately 95% of all sexual encounters end in orgasm for men. Men often measure their own sexual prowess, therefore, by applying the same criteria to their spouses.

In one of the few pieces of public data available from the US equivalent of NATSAL, called the National Survey of Sexual Health and Behavior, 85% of men said that their female partners had enjoyed an orgasm during their last sexual encounter, while only 64% of women said that they had actually had an orgasm. Someone is not telling the truth, and it's almost certainly because the women don't want to hurt the men's feelings or cannot believe (with some grounds) that men could ever understand what they want.

This is hardly an incidental question. If sex is selfless, always focused on the other person, it is right and proper and entirely Christian that couples should be asking this question and working out an answer for themselves. Should a wife have an orgasm every time? We will shortly apply our principles to try to answer this question, but before we do, we need a brief trip back to the biology classroom.

THE WONDER DOWN UNDER

Compared to the female sexual organs, a man is relatively straightforward. He is mostly (though not entirely) external. A woman is just about the opposite, and it is important to understand some basic facts about female physiology in order to grapple well with this important question. We're not going to draw you any diagrams—after all, both of you have your own live model at home. But it is worth highlighting just one or two major parts. The vulva is the proper name given to the bit between a woman's legs. It is often mistakenly called the vagina (an error infamously made by Gwyneth Paltrow on her lifestyle website, Goop), though in fact this is the muscular tube that leads from the vulva to the uterus. At the top of the vulva—as you look at it from the front or in a mirror—is the clitoris.

It's hard to see it in a non-aroused state as it hides beneath a small hood. It's a remarkable organ with a very similar physiology to a male penis: it has a tip, called a glans, and a shaft. Whereas both of these are external in a male, in a woman they are mostly hidden from view. In fact the shaft extends down into the body, shaped somewhat like a boomerang, and then splits into two (like a wishbone), with the two parts lying underneath the labia (the sets of lips that make up the opening of the vulva). Women have known about the clitoris for... well... for ever. But the medical establishment has been slower on the uptake. Before it ever inspired a hit TV show, *Gray's Anatomy* was (and still is) a medical textbook first published in 1858 and now in its 40th edition. As late as 1948, the otherwise unembarrassed editors of the book refused to label the clitoris in their section on female genitalia.

Yet this is the seat of pleasure for most women. The most sensitive parts of a woman's genitals are centred on the clitoris—the clitoral glans contains upwards of 8,000 sensory nerve endings. The labia themselves are much less sensitive and the vagina contains relatively few nerve endings. It was only in the 1960s that two American physicians, William Masters and Virginia Johnson, began to explore both the hidden anatomical delights of the female body and what actually happens in physiological terms when a woman has an orgasm. An orgasm is simply an intense sexual release. It can be triggered in all kinds of ways. Like men, women can have orgasms in their sleep or at the most unexpected moments—running up stairs in tight trousers or riding a horse or bike. You'll know it when it hits you.

For the most part, an orgasm is triggered through stimulation of the sensitive parts of the female sexual organs—the vulva (somewhat) and the clitoris (mostly). When a woman is aroused, blood flows to this external area, much as it does in a man. The labia engorge, as does the clitoris—and not just the tip, but the whole length of the shaft. As this shaft extends back into the body, it nears the wall of the vagina. At this point, the normally insensitive vaginal wall becomes more nerve-rich. This last discovery was made by Australian urologist Dr Helen O'Connell who, in 1998, effectively disproved the existence of the mythical G-spot—a magical point inside the vagina which, when stimulated, brings a woman to orgasm. This spot was named after the German doctor Ernst Gräfenberg (who also developed the IUD contraceptive device). He claimed to have discovered the spot in the 1950s.

It was a misdirection, however. For most women, depending on their physiology, the base of the clitoral shaft reaches down near to the vaginal wall. When she is aroused, stimulation here can help a woman achieve an orgasm. But there's almost certainly no magical spot, and the majority of effective stimulation is always external. We've just answered another of the questions Christians ask, by the way!

Because of this God-given design, only a minority of women achieve an orgasm through penetrative sex alone. Estimates vary but it is generally thought the percentage of women who can do this is around 20%. Even then, the data is somewhat misleading. In 1920, Princess Maria Bonaparte, great grand-niece of the first French Emperor Napoleon himself, conducted some very unscientific studies which concluded that there was a link between the ability to have a penetrative orgasm and the distance between the clitoris and the vagina (which varies from woman to woman). She was so persuaded by her own results that she had surgery to move her own clitoris nearer her vaginal opening. It was, unsurprisingly, unsuccessful.

However, her research has been rerun under more scientific conditions as recently as 2010 by two US Physicians, Kim Wallen and Elisabeth A. Lloyd. Their research is publicly available in the US National Library of Medicine archive and it confirms Maria Bonaparte's hypothesis—there is indeed a link between the two. The nearer the clitoris is to the vaginal opening, the more likely a woman is to achieve an orgasm through penetrative intercourse. In other words, even for those who achieve orgasms in this way, the reason is still almost certainly external stimulation of the clitoris which, being nearer, is more likely to be touched or rubbed by the pubic bone or penis of a partner during sex.

Your biology teacher may or may not have explained all this to you. We're old enough that neither of ours did, but you can now find this in the most basic books about sexual health. But before you get your ruler out and start measuring your most intimate parts, accept that the chances are that a wife already knows what is most likely to make her come. Why not, men, simply ask? It is surprising how few couples really understand how each other's bodies work. Indeed, they are even in the dark about what arouses their partner, and this lack of communication can be deadly when it comes to maintaining and delighting in the sexual intimacy that God has granted us to enjoy.

WHAT'S NORMAL?

Just before we apply our principles, we need to use some data to help us set a good context. The UK surveys over the last three decades have not asked women whether or how often they achieved orgasms as part of sex with their partner. But the US surveyors displayed no such reservations. Their findings are backed up by plenty of other surveys which vary somewhat but show the same broad tendency. The graph summarises the situation, with data taken from the 1992 US national survey.

Just half of women who responded said that they regularly experienced orgasms during sex. A quarter of women said they never achieved orgasms. This surprisingly high figure needs to be read alongside the figures for women's contentment with sex. In the NATSAL survey, contentment was as high as 87%. The two questions have not been put together in national surveys, but it is possible to see a very important conclusion—not every woman achieves orgasms every time, *and for some that doesn't matter.* Men struggle with this finding, driven as they are by their own experience of sexual release. But study after study has revealed the same truth: *an orgasm is not necessarily the ultimate goal for every sexual act for every woman,* amazing though it is. That reality needs to shape some of your thinking.

% OF WOMEN WHO EXPERIENCED ORGASM DURING SEX
US 1992 NHSLS

LET'S DO IT

First of all, we need to apply the goodness and joyfulness of sex to the question of orgasms for women. A female climax is neither sinful nor dirty. Indeed, enjoyment is one of the reasons that God has given married couples the gift of sexual intimacy. Christ "enjoys" the church, she brings him pleasure and delight. The church certainly enjoys him. Let's not be frightened of things making us happy.

And just because the world seems to be obsessed with orgasms, that doesn't mean Christians should ignore them. In God's good design, he has made the female body with a part like no other—just for enjoyment. The clitoris serves no other function that we are aware of. Most animals also have a clitoris, though in many the urethra (from where you pee) passes through it, just like in the male penis. However, the clitoris seems to serve a different function in animals, providing a point of arousal to make mating possible rather than enjoyable.

Humans, it seems, are altogether different. It's clear in the Song of Songs that Mrs Solomon is anticipating the joy of sexual union with her husband. She's not dreading it, nor simply lying back and "thinking of England"—although in her case, it would presumably be Israel she is contemplating. No, the goodness of sex means that God has made it for her to enjoy, as well as her spouse.

Most women understand that this enjoyment comes in different ways. The closeness and intimacy of sex generally means more to a wife than it does to a husband; similarly, the delight of touching and holding carry much more weight in a woman's enjoyment than they do for most men. Yet an orgasm is something quite different; it is a pure moment of sexual ecstasy and joy; a moment of forgotten inhibitions and overwhelming pleasure. It's part of God's design and so we should not ignore, neglect or belittle it in our Christian marriages. Couples who feel positively about orgasms, seeing them as a healthy part of marriage, are on the right track. Those who are embarrassed or find such exuberance distasteful have yet to discover all the goodness that God has planned for a husband and wife to enjoy together.

KEEP TAKING THE TABLETS

Can we apply the preventative nature of sex to the female orgasm? We think it's possible. If a woman feels unfulfilled in herself, she is on dangerous ground. There is plenty of evidence to suggest that women do not seek out extra-marital affairs at the same rate as disenchanted men, but it does happen. More likely, she is going to be tempted to seek the comforts that sex brings, but in other ways. As we have just noted, women are not motivated just by orgasms. They are moved by closeness, intimacy and emotional connection too. The temptations they face are that if their husbands do not consider their needs in the bedroom, they may be tempted to find substitutes elsewhere.

NATSAL data shows an increase in solo sex (masturbation) among men *and* women. Moreover, though use of pornography is high among men (even Christian men), neither is it insignificant among women. Porn is not just a male issue. Couples where either the husband or the wife pursue such an activity must ask serious questions about whether their sex life really is as preventative as God has ordained it to be.

It would be churlish to suggest that a lack of orgasms is going to lead straight to marital infidelity or even emotional adultery (where one spouse forms unhelpful non-sexual relationships with members of the opposite sex). But being happy in the bedroom, in all its complexity, is still preventative for both men and women. Orgasms may not be your ultimate desire, but if you want to come and don't, or your husband does not give you a chance to, the dissatisfaction, frustration and possibly anger you will feel is going to have a detrimental effect on your marriage, your home and your other relationships.

IT'S NOT ABOUT YOU

Many men labour under the misapprehension that without an orgasm their wife has really not enjoyed sex at all. Best-selling books such as *She Comes First* by US doctor Ian Kerner have only served to reinforce the stereotype. Kerner claims that we need to reject thinking of stimulating the clitoris as *foreplay* and instead rethink it as *coreplay*—something that is integral to every sexual act. When a wife rejects such advances, a husband can assume there must be something wrong with him or that he is simply not a very good lover. No doubt Kerner and others like him are responding to the kind of male-centric sex that dominated much of life until the last 50 years or so and are offering a kind of correction. But they're doing couples no favours by establishing patterns which aren't always what women want.

There's a flip side to this principle which speaks to women. It is quite possible—especially in the glossy-magazine climate which also seeks to make an orgasm the only measure of good sex—for women to become extraordinarily demanding of their husbands. Our principle holds that sex is not about the husband's gratification for the husband—but neither is about the wife's for the wife. Sex for her is about serving her husband and it is possible to ignore this truth in the pursuit of an elusive moment. Happily, most men are willing to help their wives come. It is a language they understand! They might not be very good at it, and may need help holding back, but few are not excited by the challenge.

LET'S TALK ABOUT IT

Once again, every couple needs to understand the importance of communication when it comes to this issue. We have seen what a great variety of responses there are: from women who want to—and do—have an orgasm every time through to those who hardly ever, or even never, experience an orgasm. Moreover, within these last two groups, some want to come, and some don't.

What is true in the general is also true in the specific. When a married couple make love, it is pretty much a sure fire bet that the husband wants to reach a climax, but you can't necessarily say the same about a wife, even if it is part of her normal response. Female sexuality and arousal are a lot more complex for women than for men, who have a helpful or annoying tendency (depending on your point of view) to be able to compartmentalise life and concentrate on just one thing.

How is a couple ever going to reach such a happy arrangement unless they talk about it? Put more bluntly, it is good for a husband to ask his wife, "Do you want to come?" And it's ok for her to say, "Yes" or "No" and for the husband not to feel any sense of success or failure as a result. This talking needs to extend to technique. We've already seen that some women are able to achieve an orgasm through penetrative sex alone, although it is a minority. For those who cannot, it is absolutely critical for a husband and wife to talk about what helps or hinders the process. There is no need for prudishness, this is not a public conversation; it's not going to be repeated anywhere else. Make sure both of you know what works and what does not and be happy with it.

KEEP THE DOOR CLOSED

You will have noticed that we've started to apply our last principle to this subject. The value of the various data we have looked at is that we have established there is no one-size fits all approach for women. Unlike with men, there is no standard by which sex is measurable—and we certainly should not let the presence or otherwise of an orgasm be that measure. What is right for you is right for you. No one else and no other couple are your measure. For some women, an orgasm every time is the norm and the measure of good sex. Husbands have got to accommodate that desire into their serving. For others it is less necessary or even elusive. For some of these wives, it will matter a great deal. For others it will be a matter of indifference. Again, husbands have to serve well.

What matters is whether it is good for you as a couple. Is sex what God intended it to be for you? What brings you *closer*? Never mind what Julie or Jeff are doing in their bedroom, nor what *Cosmopolitan* is telling you. How are you serving one another? It's your business.

BRINGING EVERYTHING TO A CLIMAX

Now we've helped you to answer two questions, it may be time to take stock. For questions we have about sex are rarely asked in isolation. Take these first two. If you are a once-a-week kind of couple (just above national average, if you're interested), then each intimate occasion may be extraordinarily intense. You may be more likely, if you're a woman, to desire or achieve an orgasm every time.

If you're a once-a-day couple you're in the top four per cent of married couples, but don't get cocky—it's quality and not just quantity that counts. If that does describe you, then it is more likely that some of that sex will be basic no-frills intimacy (if there is such a thing). It's much less likely statistically that a wife will want to have an orgasm every time. Frequency and orgasmic activity are therefore not unrelated. In both cases, you've got to find your happy place and rejoice in it, in each other, and being joined together as one. For that is, after all, why God has given you this amazing gift.

We get *closer* by delighting in the other person's happiness, wants and desires. Christ gave himself for us. And the church lives to please him. The meaningfulness of sex, therefore, is directly linked to this other-person centredness and satisfaction.

Q3: THE OTHER BIG O

IS IT OK FOR CHRISTIANS TO
HAVE ORAL SEX?

In late 2017, an internet meme about oral sex went viral on social media. It was a chart made up of a list of 18 American states where oral sex was still illegal, together with the maximum permissible punishment in each one. States included Florida, Texas and Virginia and the punishment ranged from a large fine of several thousand dollars to a custodial prison sentence. Like much of what you can read on the internet, the meme turned out to be fake news. A Supreme Court ruling in 2003 (Lawrence v Texas) made all the statutes on oral sex and its legality redundant. Oral sex is legal everywhere in the USA, whatever the internet may tell you.

Mind you, not everyone thinks it counts as sex.

Famously—or rather, infamously—Bill Clinton claimed "not to have had sex with that woman" referring to Monica Lewinsky when they had participated in oral sex together. Some teenagers and unmarried Christians still try to make a case for oral sex not being "real sex" and therefore not problematic for those who are unwed. We trust you won't make the same error: whether you decide it is right or wrong for you, it is clearly intimate, private and joins a couple together in many of the same ways vaginal intercourse does. It belongs, therefore (if it belongs anywhere) in marriage alone.

It's a perplexing question for Christians. They just don't know what to think about it. Perhaps it is something they enjoy, but feel guilty about. Others don't know whether to give it a try. Others still, don't like it, and worry that they don't. We call it "the other big O" as it's an area that many have questions about but are simply too embarrassed to ask. Perhaps it's no surprise then that when US pastor and teacher John Piper celebrated the 400th edition of his podcast "Ask Pastor John" this is the very issue he tackled. The interviewer promised listeners that such a milestone "should be marked with an epic episode" and—based on the number of questions asked—this is the topic they chose to address. His answer is good and thorough, as you might expect, but we want to show you that our five biblical principles will do an equally good job of (if you'll forgive the pun) putting this issue to bed for you.

Let's get technical for a moment so we know what we're talking about. Oral sex is actually two different things: fellatio is when a wife performs oral sex on her husband (from the Latin verb *fello* meaning "to suck"). Cunnilingus is the reverse (from the two Latin words *cunna* and *lingo* meaning "vulva" and "to lick or tap lightly with the tongue"). The terms are self-explanatory. Both terms, while being technically accurate, are rather cold and mechanistic. We think it is better to think about it in terms of kissing with the "kisses of the mouth" to use the term from Song of Songs 1 v 2—all over the body, not just mouth-to-mouth.

Historically, oral sex is as old as civilization, widely known in ancient cultures judging by many of the depictions of it that exist. One curious exception was the Greco-Roman context into which many Bible letters were written, where it was generally considered a taboo. That is surprising given that so many other sexual practices were tolerated and even celebrated, for example sodomy (see the next question) but it might go some way to explaining its complete absence from any New Testament writings. However, as with other questions, our whole strategy is to apply Bible principles to *any* question—whether or not it gets a Scriptural mention. Let's do that now.

LET'S DO IT

NATSAL2 was conducted in 2000 and found that 86% of married men and 81% of married women had performed oral sex on their partner in the last year. The data was not separated out for married or single people in the 2010 survey so it's more difficult to draw conclusions, but it seems highly unlikely that the data is lower a decade on. Once the effect of answers from those over 45 is stripped out (for whom the percentages tail off), then the proportions are even higher. As Christians, however, we need a slightly better answer to the question than simply "Everyone is doing it". The data is a help in so far as it goes—this hardly seems a niche activity (spot the difference in the next chapter when we discuss anal sex). But to see whether oral sex fits into our definition of sex as good, holy and pure we need to dig a little deeper.

Let's start with that most explicit of books, the Song of Songs. Even here, things are not immediately clear. Hebrew is a fabulously euphemistic language using subtle expressions to describe all kinds of bodily functions. Once you know that "covering the feet", for example, can mean to have a bowel movement, and that "feet" are sometimes a euphemism for the genitals, there are some parts of Scripture you may never read the same way again! The challenge for us is that these phrases don't always mean the same. Sometimes feet are really just feet! We have to allow the context to shape our understanding.

Let's take another Hebrew word—the word for navel. It's not a common word in the Bible and one of the few places it occurs clearly refers to the umbilical cord (see Ezekiel 16 v 4). But think a little more deeply—the cord is attached to a baby's belly button, but emerges from the mother's birth canal, and so it should not surprise us that the word can also mean—depending on its setting—a woman's vulva. What does this do for a reading of Song of Songs 7 v 2, "Your navel is a rounded goblet that never lacks blended wine"? Some commentators argue that the passage demands that we understand this in its more intimate way. After all, the gaze of Solomon is moving up his wife's body and the sentence before describes her legs and the one after her waist. The belly button would come after both of those, not between them. And so, he says, it makes most sense to see Solomon anticipating the "blended wine", as being of the most intimate vintage, not her navel fluff. Not everyone agrees. One commentator tends to see the most explicit meanings in each ambiguity, but others play this down and take us away from the intimacy of the most private of areas into the relative safety of whether Mrs S has an "inny" or an "outy". Who knows?

Equally, there are no direct references in Song of Songs to fellatio. Some of those who want to force the issue see layers of meaning in verses such as 2 v 3, "Like an apple tree among the trees of the forest is my beloved among the young men. I delight to sit in his shade, and his fruit is sweet to my taste." They may be right, but Mrs Solomon might equally simply be saying she quite fancies this Solomon guy. It's just impossible to come to a conclusion. You may wish that the book was all together clearer, but remember this is love poetry, not *The Joy of (Ancient) Sex*. It's supposed to be subtle and indirect.

What we can be clear about is this: Solomon and his bride give themselves fully to one another and seem to hold nothing back. There is no part of Solomon that Mrs S does not admire. There is no part of his bride that the groom is not head-over-heels in love with. They shower each other with kisses. They touch and caress. Neither seems embarrassed by this closeness. There don't seem to be off-limit areas, as they (to use Paul's vocabulary) yield themselves to one another. So, although there is no explicit mention, oral sex does not seem to be either against the content or the tone of this love poem.

But is it a healthy practice? Is it dangerous in any way? In 2013, Hollywood actor Michael Douglas, now married to fellow thespian Catherine Zeta-Jones, revealed that he had almost died from throat cancer. He claimed that the cancer was not a result of his heavy smoking habit but rather through contracting HPV (human papillomavirus) by having oral sex with other women.

HPV (which women in the UK are now immunised against at school age) is indeed one of the causes of throat cancer (though in this case not the most likely given Douglas's nicotine addiction). While oral sex is no different from other forms of sex when it comes to the possibility of transmission of HPV, researchers estimate that it is significantly more likely to be actually communicated through vaginal or anal sex than oral sex. So it is incorrect to write off oral sex as "bad for you" simply on the basis of this rather sensational story, without also writing off all other kinds of sexual intimacy.

We do have to say, however, that there are certain practices that seem to count as oral sex in some people's minds which Christians *must* write off. It is impossible to escape the influence of pornography here. There are forms of oral sex which are aggressive and abusive. Forgive the directness, but we need to say that such forms of fellatio (for it is normally that way around), which include forceful grabbing of the head or other similar practices are clearly *not* good and are contrary to nearly every one of the principles we have established.

KEEP TAKING THE TABLETS

So far, we have seen that our first principle doesn't seem to rule out oral sex, but equally we could say that it doesn't rule it in either. Does our second help us make progress? Sexual intimacy, remember, is a God-given gift to married couples to protect them against the evil and immorality that is in the world. Up to now, we have suggested that it does this by—to put it bluntly—stopping either of the couple looking elsewhere. We have also said that while this reasoning doesn't sound very romantic, it is actually extremely so, as it preserves faithfulness and removes temptation. One of the best romantic and spiritual things we can do for our spouse is to help them not fall into temptation.

This protection also serves a positive purpose. Physical closeness builds connection and trust. That's true at any level—think of the hug a kind Christian gave you after a service when you were feeling low. It's also true at the most intimate of levels: closeness between a naked husband and wife touching, feeling, caressing, kissing all over. Such intimacy builds connection and trust for a couple or is an expression of an already existing trust in a way that a trip to the local cinema, fun though it is, can never be. If marriages are to prosper, there needs to be this kind of closeness.

It is also worth reflecting that oral sex *can* (notice we avoid the word *ought*) help with mismatched libido. This is one of the hardest issues to reconcile within a marriage—what happens when one of you wants sex more than the other? Should the more highly-sexed partner (usually, though not always the man) always get their way? Should the one with lower desires be able to dictate terms? One way to answer this question is to realise that sexual intimacy does not always need to mean penetrative intercourse. Intimacy takes many forms, ranging from kissing and cuddling, through to the more obvious. Oral sex, some couples find, can help them find a happy balance that serves both partners and keeps the flame alive.

There are also sometimes seasons where penetrative sex is difficult. Most couples who are married long enough find that they have these at some point; if that's you right now, then you really are Mr and Mrs Normal. These may be times of illness, physical or mental; they may be times of stress (though sex is a remarkably good de-stressor). Many couples feel uncomfortable enjoying sex during a wife's period: if you're the once-a-week couple you may be able to cope with that; if you're the once-a-day minority, you will have to either be patient or find some other ways to enjoy intimacy. Oral sex can be part of the solution to these kinds of seasons though it does need both of you to agree.

IT'S NOT ABOUT YOU

Nowhere is it more pressing for us to recover the mutuality of sex than in the area of oral sex. Let's face it: most men like it. (For the record, so do most women, but the overall percentages are lower, and the percentages of women who like it *all* the time are *much, much* lower). This mutuality, remember, is the husband fulfilling his duty to his wife and the wife to her husband. It is the wife yielding her body to her husband and the husband yielding his body to her. It is seeking the good of the other before yourself, putting that great Christian principle (Philippians 2 v 4) into practice in the bedroom.

However, we have also seen that the principle is more nuanced than that. We cannot—for example—demand that a spouse does something for us in order to fulfil his or her side of the bargain. Sex is not a negotiation or a transaction. Nor is it a tit-for-tat "I'll do this for you if you do this for me". So, at the two extremes, no spouse can demand that their partner engages in fellatio or cunnilingus. But we also need to say that no spouse should use the principle as a power of veto.

Where does that leave us? For some readers, this question is easily answered. You both like it and that's fine. Or you both don't. And that's fine too. If you both think it is ok, a good or honourable part of your love life, your only question is about who gets to go first, and even that is easily fixed, because you may have discovered it's not a choice you have to make—we'll let you work that one out.

What, however, if you disagree? What happens when one of you wants it, and the other doesn't? Your reasons may be varied, but the mismatch is real. Let's try to apply our principle. First, let's speak to the eager partner. Sex, remember, is not about you. It is about you yielding your body to your spouse and giving him or her authority over it. How does that shape your desire for oral sex? It should have a profound effect on you. In fact, you should learn to delight in what your spouse *doesn't like* as much as what he or she does.

And for the reluctant partner? When you share these intimate moments with your partner you are yielding to them, letting them have authority over you. At that moment it is not about you, it is about them, and you being happy with them being happy.

This is not quite the whole story, however. We're back to Laurel and Hardy trying to jam themselves through the door at the same time. So, these two attitudes need to come together to create a sense in which sex is about learning to love what the other one loves. It is not about toleration or endurance. It is about genuinely loving what your spouse loves.

LET'S TALK ABOUT IT

You may think by now that we're living in an alternative reality where all these differences can be ironed out magically by simply saying to one another, "Your call, darling". Nothing could be further from the truth. The mutuality of sex demands more than simply deferring to the other. Nonetheless, it's impossible to make progress in this area unless a couple can talk about it. When it comes to this most private of subjects, that communication needs to include talking about what we like and what we don't. It needs honesty and courage to say why something is good or why it is difficult. It needs trust to know that conversations that happen in the bedroom won't go beyond. All this is good communication.

Every Saturday, the *The Times* newspaper carries an advice column by sexologist Suzi Godson. It doesn't matter what the problem, the solution is always, at some level, to talk about it. Learning to share with each other is a key part of learning to be married, yet it is surprising how many couples are able to be open and honest about nearly every subject (holidays, kids, cars, houses, work, church) except sex. And when it comes to oral sex that situation is exacerbated as no one wants to be the killjoy and no one wants to force themselves on their beloved partner.

The world's best-known Christian relationship and parenting expert is Kevin Leman. Many of his books are very helpful if you really do need step-by-step guides to intimacy. In his book, *Under the Sheets*, he says that good communication is the best-kept secret to super sex. In fact, he claims, "most couples spend 1 percent of their sexual relationship talking about it and 99 percent making love". He suggests the percentage should be nearer 90 percent talking and 10 percent doing. He's got a point. In his book, he includes a little oral sex "true or false" quiz for couples. This is not to test their knowledge of fellatio, but to see whether "oral sex is for you". It might seem rather contrived, but it is useful in at least one sense. Towards the end of the questionnaire, he points out that the most important thing is that you talk and agree. Good sex needs good communication. Working a way through your own answer to this question requires the best sort of all.

KEEP THE DOOR CLOSED

It is, however, your own way. You may already know your own answer, or you may be itching to hear Pastor John's answer to this question. For what it's worth, he's coming up with the same conclusion as us: is oral sex OK? Maybe, maybe not. Sure, it's not prohibited in Scripture and it may do you a lot of good. But it may not. It all depends. And, he says, in a "biblically beautiful marriage both of [you should] seek to outdo the other in showing kindness".

It's quite possible you've flicked to this part of the book first to see what we have to say about this subject. Maybe you were hoping we would rule oral sex out. Maybe you were hoping we'd rule it in. Our answer is neither. Instead, we're asking you to work through these principles together and come to a loving but private decision about what makes you *closer*. You don't need to worry about legality. But you do need to worry about each other and what will build and cement the wonderful marriage that God has so graciously given you.

Q4: A IS FOR...

IS IT OK FOR CHRISTIANS TO HAVE ANAL SEX?

Twenty years ago, most Christians would have completed this sentence exactly the same way. A is for Apple. Now, especially if you were talking about sex, the answers would be different. The whole question of anal sex was not really on any Christian's radar—and it certainly didn't feature in the top-ten questions people ask. All that has changed. And the change is almost entirely down to two major factors. First, the influence of the pornography culture we find ourselves immersed in today has normalised many behaviours that were previously seen as taboo. If ever portrayed in movies, anal sex was almost certainly shown in a negative abusive way (most famously perhaps Marlon Brando's notorious and disturbing scene with Maria Schneider in *Last Tango in Paris*). Second, the societal acceptance of homosexuality, particularly male homosexuality, has made anal sex more of an acceptable cultural practice even if it is still relatively rare in heterosexual relationships.

These two factors have combined to make the topic of anal sex not quite mainstream, exactly, but certainly one that people are interested in and asking questions about, Christians included. In March 2017, this switch into the mainstream intensified when Hollywood actress and lifestyle guru Gwyneth Paltrow, announced via her Goop website that it was a practice she herself enjoyed. Suddenly newspaper and magazine articles were openly discussing the topic in ways they had been cagey about doing so before.

Most secular books on sex now contain sections on anal sex without any question as to its validity or appropriateness for a couple. Nevertheless, we need to understand that it still remains a minority activity. The chart shows the responses in the UK national surveys to the question "Have you had anal intercourse in the last twelve months?" That's a fairly long timescale, but even so, in 2010 less than 15% of all men and only 10% of all women answered in the affirmative. Moreover—and this is one of the main surprises of the 2010 survey—the number of women answering yes declined since the previous survey a decade earlier.

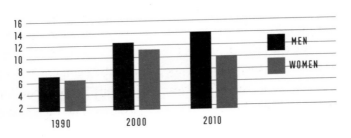

% ENGAGED IN ANAL SEX AT LEAST ONCE LAST YEAR
SOURCE: NATSAL 1,2,3

The most famous of all sexual surveys was carried out by Alfred Kinsey in the 1940s and 1950s. In his published data he made no mention of anal sex, but when the full research was finally published some 40 years later it turned out that Kinsey, who was obsessed with unusual or deviant behaviour, had asked a similar question. Responses were so low, however, to be completely meaningless and he omitted the research from any public announcements. So, we are asking a question here about what has been and remains a minority activity. Compare this to the data we presented in the last chapter about oral sex—80-90% for married couples. But it's still a question Christians have and therefore, as it makes it into the top ten, we're going to try to help you answer it using the five principles. This will be a shorter section, however, because— spoiler alert!—we think the answer is fairly straightforward.

LET'S DO IT

Sex, remember, is a good and holy gift from a gracious Father for married couples. It binds them together, building intimacy and trust. How does this stack up with the reality of anal sex for couples? The well-respected British Medical Journal (BMJ) reported research in 2014 which summarised the effect that anal sex had on women: it "often appeared to be painful, risky and coercive". All three words should ring alarm bells for believers. Lauren Streicher, Director of the Center for Sexual Medicine and Menopause at the Feinberg School of Medicine in the US is clear: "The anus is not made for sex. It's supposed to be a one-way passage". The vagina, she points out, has a thick, elastic outer wall, ideal for both sex and childbirth. The anus wall, on the other hand, is relatively thin and inelastic, so inserting anything into it runs the risk of tearing and permanent damage. It produces insufficient natural lubrication.

Most transmissions of HPV (see the last question and answer for actor Michael Douglas's story) happen through anal sex and Dr. Streicher recently reported a new study from her university (Northwestern) where women who regularly engaged in anal sex reported incidences of both urinary and faecal incontinence. The top medical journal for those interested in sexuality is *The Journal of Sexual Medicine*. Articles are restricted for mere amateurs like you and us, but you can scan through the titles of the research papers for the last few years. What you would discover is that there are more articles about the negative effects of anal sex (and how they can be mitigated) than almost any other topic. The American Cancer Society reports quite clearly that anal sex increases the risk of anal cancer. Put simply, the evidence is strong and compelling—*it's not very good for you.*

In biblical terms, you can't really make a precise case one way or another. Some point to examples of sodomy in the Bible (for example in Genesis 19). While sodomy today has come to mean any form of anal sex, in the Bible the practice was exclusively homosexual, so it is difficult to draw any conclusions about heterosexual activity. What about in the wider world? In the UK, the country where we live, anal sex between consenting opposite sex adults was illegal when we got married in 1991 and it was not until 1994 that the Criminal Justice and Public Order Act made it permissible. Even then, it was illegal for those under 18, though the sexual age of consent and marriage was 16. The limit was not reduced until 2000. Unlike oral sex, therefore (which UK law has never banned for married couples), anal sex has been treated quite differently, recognising something of its destructive nature.

Taken together, none of this is a pretty picture and seems to be a world away from the language of good or holy. Though we have been careful to let you find your answers to each of the questions we have posed so far, this particular issue seems to us to be much clearer. Anal sex hardly seems to fit into the pattern of intimacy and celebration of oneness that God has established for married couples. In case you are not yet persuaded, it also, we believe, breaks some of our other principles.

KEEP TAKING THE TABLETS

How might anal sex protect a couple? Could you make an argument, for example, that anal sex, much like oral sex, prevents immorality? If a couple were not able to enjoy vaginal sex for some reason or other, might not anal sex be a good alternative to prevent Satan tempting them (to borrow Paul's Corinthians phrase)?

We think that this is something you need to discuss yourselves, but it seems to us that this question is a little perverse because it assumes too much. Based on our previous answer, we cannot see that anal sex is a *good* alternative even though it is unarguably *an* alternative. Given that there are other solutions to this particular question, such a remedy seems unnecessary. Moreover, there is a double perversity because if, as we have suggested, the increased popularity of anal sex is a result of the influence of pornography and/or the acceptance of homosexuality, then far from protecting from sexual immorality (1 Corinthians 7 v 2), anal sex brings it right into the bedroom.

IT'S NOT ABOUT YOU

We need to be honest and say that in almost every case, anal sex is something men want, rather than what women want. There's plenty of evidence to support this claim. One instance is the anomalous reduction in women engaging in anal sex (see chart above). They want it less because they like it less. But there is also plenty of research to back up the idea that anal sex comes from a male-orientated world, one of sexual dominance. The best study we've seen was published in the *Perspectives on Sexual and Reproductive Health Journal* in 2017. It found that anal sex, where it occurred, was initiated by men 82% of the time. As other non-scientific studies have found, women simply don't like it.

The selfless principle we have established is not a permission to demand from a spouse anything you want. It's not "She has to, because she has given me authority". The yielding of the body is mutual—husband to wife, wife to husband. It's very difficult indeed to see how a one-sided practice liked by some men, but almost universally hated by women, is acceptable on this basis.

LET'S TALK ABOUT IT

Hang on a minute. Didn't Gwyneth like it? Or at least, that is what she suggested. If anal sex is initiated by men 82% of the time, isn't it initiated by women 18% of the time? Both these facts are incontrovertibly true, but pure statistics are not enough. What if Gwyneth is embracing anal sex only because she wants her partner to like her? What if the 18% only initiate anal sex because—despite their horror of the "pain and risk" (BMJ) they want to keep their man? We're not suggesting we know whether either suggestion is true or not, we're just suggesting that there may be more to headlines than meet the eye.

You are never going to know the answer to those questions without good, clear and honest communication. Talking about sex needs to include more than "what" questions and embrace "why" questions too: motive is important here. A husband who coerces his wife into anal sex by getting her to initiate it is hardly yielding his body or authority to her, nor is he allowing her to do so for him. He is totally in control. And that is not beautiful, biblical sex; that is abuse.

KEEP THE DOOR CLOSED

Of course, there are going to be exceptions to each of these data points, and maybe—just maybe—you're the exception.

Frankly, we doubt it; but that's for you to talk about and work out for yourself. Ultimately, even our strong suggestion is only that. We've yet to come across a situation where anal sex is a healthy part of loving sanctification, bringing couples *closer*. But we are not you, and you are a couple accountable together, for each other, before God. We can't decide this issue for you.

Q5: I COULD DO WITH SOME HELP HERE...

WHAT SHOULD WE THINK ABOUT SEX AIDS?

U K website Lovehoney operates a warehouse in Bath, England 24/7. It ships over 10,000 items worldwide *every month*. And this site is just one of many catering for the same market: sex aids of one kind or another.

Christians are rightly wary about visiting some of these websites because of what they might come across, and so in recent years, Christian versions of the same online shopping experience have sprung up promising nudity-free zones and Christian-appropriate items only (whatever that means; *who decides?*). Even these so-called Christian sites fail to get past our internet filters at home. Is the subject of sex aids taboo for believers?

Couples who ask questions about sex aids generally fall into two camps: there are those who are having trouble with sex and want help; then there are others who enjoy intimacy but want it to be even better. Typically, the former would want to ask questions about sex *aids*, the latter have queries about sex *toys*, but for our purposes we can group them all together under the former slightly broader category.

Instinctively, we (and you) probably think that some aids are ok, without even applying the principles to them. So, for example, if sex is uncomfortable, perhaps because of age, time of the month or other physical reasons, there are not many Christians who would think that using a tube of lubrication was somehow wrong or even sinful. Similarly, although the medicines Viagra (*sildenafil*) or Cialis (*tadalafil*) have become known as "sex drugs" to enhance and prolong erections, both are registered for use to treat debilitating erectile dysfunction and few can object to their proper purpose given under the guidance of a physician.

The NATSAL surveyors asked a very detailed set of questions to respondents to identify those who had suffered a period of difficulties of three months or more in the last year. This is more than a casual "we couldn't do it one night" but trying to work out what proportion of the population struggled with sustained difficulties. The percentage of those who experienced actual physical pain during sex might seem relatively low—2% for men, 7% for women. (Although if you're in this minority, we recognise that these can be distressing and desperate situations.) However, the data for other common complaints are surprisingly high:

DIFFICULTY/AGE RANGE	25-34	35-44	45-54	55-64	65-74
TROUBLE MAINTAINING OR ACHIEVING AN ERECTION	8%	8%	13%	23%	30%
NO ORGASM (FOR WOMEN)	17%	14%	15%	16%	14%
UNCOMFORTABLY DRY VAGINA	10%	8%	14%	27%	20%

When the information is gathered together and analysed, the response to how many people experience prolonged difficulty in one or more area (of which these are just three) was 42% for all men and 51% of all women. That means that if you are experiencing sustained difficulty, you are not alone. And it's not wrong to ask for help.

Take erectile dysfunction as just one example: one local family doctor told us that he sees at least one new patient *every day* with this issue, but each comes to him apologetically, thinking they are the first person to pluck up the courage to seek help. He is able to reassure them that they are not as unusual as they think, and help is available.

The question of sex aids is therefore more nuanced than simply "Are they ok or not?" We probably need to ask more probing questions about the exact circumstances behind each desire to use them. We find it helpful, therefore, to think about sex aids in three categories.

There are those which *make sex possible*. These might include treatment for erectile dysfunction, or lubricants to help overcome dryness or foreskin problems. Then there are aids which aim to *make sex better*. This is probably the broadest category and might range from wearing a favourite perfume or a pair of smart Calvin Klein boxer shorts, through to vibrators or clitoral rings that stimulate the clitoris during sex. Then, finally, there are aids which *make sex redundant*. These would also include vibrators, especially vaginal ones, or artificial vaginas, which seek to replicate the sexual organs.

As we work through this chapter, we are going to focus most of our effort on the second category, which seems to us the most difficult to come to a conclusion about. Those which make sex possible should probably be seen—for the most part, anyway—in the same way we would think of other medical or relationship difficulties and therefore pose few problems for believers.

Those which make sex redundant are equally straightforward. Sexual intimacy is a connection between two individuals and replacing one of them with an artificial substitute means you are operating outside of God's given pattern. This is especially true for vaginal vibrators, which replicate the penis, often with a clitoral stimulator attached. These are known as rabbit vibrators. As Christian sex advisors often point out, it is not just that these items make sex redundant, they change the very nature of the sexual organs so as to make real loving with a spouse inferior. Most are larger than the average penis which doesn't—you may have noticed—vibrate at 1,000 RPM. The real thing ends up being less desirable. Headlines in the secular press like "Why I Love My Vibrator" should alert us to this danger.

Nevertheless, eliminating these two outlier categories still leaves us with a complex middle ground. For example, on her blog *To Love, Honor and Vacuum*, writer Sheila Wray Gregoire helpfully sets out the ways in which sex connects married couples together. The intimacy of sex, she argues, builds connections that are physical, emotional and spiritual. Sex, she says, works best when all three are involved. This is sexual sanctification. The trouble with sex aids is that they focus on the physical at the expense of the other two. Moreover, it's quite possible for a husband and wife to use a vibrator to stimulate the clitoris, but for the wife to end up "making love to the vibrator and not her husband".

We think she's right, but the question is more nuanced even than this. For while sex cannot be reduced down to a physical connection, it is not less than this either. It is not solely spiritual, nor solely emotional—you have to be in the same room for it to work. So a physical stimulant may be a help or it may be a hindrance, and that's where the principles are going to help you reach a godly conclusion.

LET'S DO IT

There are sex aids in Scripture. That's a sentence you may have never seen before in a Christian book and may never see again! But they're there nonetheless. Listen to Mrs Solomon: "While the king was at his table, my perfume spread its fragrance. My beloved is to me a sachet of myrrh resting between my breasts. My beloved is to me a cluster of henna blossoms from the vineyards of En Gedi" (Song of Songs 1 v 12-14).

Myrrh is an expensive perfume that gives off a strong scent. While henna is best known for the red dye it produces (and which our daughters use to colour their hair), it also gives off a pungent smell. Eastern women were known to secrete the blossoms about their person to draw their lovers to them. We'll let you use your own imagination to suppose exactly where they might have put them. These are sensory aphrodisiacs anticipating sex and using the anticipation to build hunger and therefore make sex better. Reading on it's possible to find both food and drink being used to intensify the experience of sex. Mrs S also puts on her best undies for her husband: "The fragrance of your garments is like the fragrance of Lebanon" he says (4 v 11). The fragrance is presumably more of the same: myrrh and henna, rather than a good measure of non-bio Persil.

In other words, it is perfectly possible for some sex aids to be part of God's good and holy plan for sexual intimacy. These helps are not to make sex possible, nor do they make sex redundant. They simply make a good thing better. To answer the broad question, God is ok with us doing this. He has given us a gift in marriage to build connection, celebrate intimacy and delight in one another. There are things we can do to treasure and deepen this gift and we ought to not be embarrassed about saying so.

Where, though, do we draw the line? Let's take Mrs S's favourite nightie. Are there garments which would be inappropriate for her to wear? So, she's wearing a little number with lace edging for her husband, but should we feel the same if she dons a sluttier outfit and dresses up to look like one of the local prostitutes? You can see, we hope, that even such simple questions as what we wear are not as simple as they first appear.

Let us develop the idea of what is good and holy. It seems to us that whether we can include sex aids in this "good" category depends on the answers to two key questions. The first is the *nature* of the aid itself. Some categories rule themselves out by nature of what they are. The second question is the *motive* for wanting to use the aid. What does it do that makes sex better or more intense?

Let's take the first of those questions. If you agree with our conclusions about anal sex in the previous chapter, then anal toys seem to fall beyond the boundary of acceptability. Equally, as we have already suggested, those which are used for vaginal penetration hardly seem to promote connection between a couple. It goes without saying that those that are illegal (for example, certain medications used in illicit ways) or aggressive, hurtful or dominating (such as bindings) should also be off-limits for Christians. Yet there will be a whole range of other objects that don't fall at this first hurdle: we would include clitoral stimulants, clothing, perfume or lotions, flavoured condoms and so on.

This is where the second question—asking about motive— becomes relevant. Take something as straightforward as some sexy underwear. Why do you or your spouse want to wear such garments? To show off your/their body just to you? That seems fine and fits with Mrs Solomon's own approach. But what if you are wearing something to transform you into something you're not. What if that thong doesn't just show off your pert derrière to your husband but makes you into a pole dancer? What if those boxer shorts don't just accentuate your torso but transform you into a member of the Chippendales dance troupe? Then suddenly, those aids are doing something different, and you're moving away from the good and holy purpose for which God gave you sexual intimacy.

KEEP TAKING THE TABLETS

Can such aids ever be preventative? Frankly, we think our second principle is rather redundant on this question. If anything, they may *promote* immorality rather than reign it in. So, perhaps we can only answer in the most general terms: sex that is intensified in godly ways, is a good thing. It draws you ever closer as a couple. It provides intimacy and connection that nothing else can. And therefore, it does sometimes keep you from the temptation that Paul is so keen that Christian couples should avoid.

IT'S NOT ABOUT YOU

Our third principle is one of the most helpful when it comes to addressing this question. We have seen that sex is about yielding ourselves to one another, granting our spouse authority over our body. If a sex aid undermines that selflessness, there is something seriously wrong going on. Sheila Wray Gregoire is exactly right here: if you start loving your sex toy and even, in her words, making love to it, then that is not really sex at all; not as God intended it to be.

The selflessness principle is also helpful in determining exactly what boundaries to draw. Many husbands like making their wives come, either using their hands or mouths. Some wives find the power or consistency of a vibrator speeds up the process. But if the husband is yielding himself to his wife, then he will be happy to wait and make sure she enjoys an orgasm, without the need for artificial stimulation. He'll delight in that. If the wife is yielding herself to her husband, then she will be happy for him to take the project on! She'll delight in his participation—and a vibrator in these circumstances fails the test.

But in another scenario, a husband might not have the stamina nor the longevity to help his wife to an orgasm. His wife might need the help that some clitoral stimulation can provide that neither she nor her husband can provide. In these circumstances, the same vibrator from the same manufacturer might pass the test as something good and positive to use.

LET'S TALK ABOUT IT

We're beginning to see the importance of honest and open communication. On the surface, couples will be unable to come to any conclusion about this question unless they talk about it. Moreover, this talk needs to be deeper than "What do you like?" We hope you can see that questions such as "Why do you like it?" are equally important. And it is critical that these questions are answered honestly between a couple, because the responses may be the difference between a positive or a negative conclusion.

Take a couple who like to dress in some nice underwear as part of their lovemaking. If a husband likes to see his wife in stockings because it makes her seem immoral or debauched, but is dishonest about his motives to his wife, then if she acquiesces to his desires, he will be coercing her to be complicit in his impure motives. No one is helped. But if he is honest about his motives and they feel that it is wrong, they can cry, repent, laugh and be restored together. Sex will probably be better as a result. Couples also need to realise that motives change over time. You should not assume that just because one of you thought something ten years ago, you still think the same today. And so—to continue the clothing example—it's ok to ask, "What would you like me to wear?" even if you think you know the answer. Communication means talking and listening over and over again.

Nor should you ignore that communication itself can be a form of sex aid. What husband is not moved by a whisper in the kitchen, "I'm wearing your favourite [...]" (fill in your own blank)? And what wife is not melted when her husband comes over to her, hugs her and tells her that she looks absolutely ravishing tonight? If all this talk of clitoral stimulation and sexy lingerie leaves you a little cold, don't worry, because words are one of the most powerful sex aids you can possibly imagine.

KEEP THE DOOR CLOSED

Just like every other area of your sex life, this is one for you to work through yourself. Because so much depends on motive, you may even find that you come to a completely different conclusion on some questions than another couple who are facing the exact same set of circumstances. But you'll never know: and that's the point. Their conclusion is not yours; and yours is not theirs. And that's just fine.

In fact, you might want to take issue with some of the more cut-and-dried conclusions we have drawn in this chapter. That is your right. We just ask that you consistently and honestly apply these Bible principles to arrive at your answers as you seek to be *closer*.

And then, keep it to yourself.

SECTION 4

The end

We've tried to make the case for husbands and wives to be closer: for sex for married Christian couples to be increasing in its meaningfulness so that it is fulfilling spiritually, physically and emotionally. Such transformation will also, we believe, make sex better. Although simple enjoyment, while good, is not our ultimate goal.

Most Christian talk about sexual sanctification tends to be in the area of "putting off"—that is, things to avoid. Good. That is needed. The casting off of sin is a key element of any pursuit of holiness. There's been lots written on this subject and we've not attempted to repeat what others have already eloquently said.

However, sanctification in any area of life is also about "putting on". And it is here that we feel Christians seem reluctant to speak about sexual intimacy. In one sense, that is unsurprising. Sex between a married couple is—rightly—a private, intimate affair; really, it's no one's business but your own before God.

Yet our failure to even vocalise the concept means that we are missing out. We are satisfied with below-standard intimacy. We tolerate a decline in its enjoyment, frequency and significance. Given everything that intimacy points to, this is a shocking oversight. Over time, many couples report that—far from moving closer together—they find themselves drifting apart.

Some Christians feel that this is a subject which should not be mentioned, let alone have a book devoted to it. At times, writing these words for you, we've felt a bit like that ourselves. Neither of us are natural extroverts, and this is not a book we want to hand to you on a crowded train platform, or in the church foyer. But we do want you to read it, because we want you to make progress as Christians in every area of life, and that means this one too.

HOW MUCH DOES SEX REALLY MATTER?

For many years Christians have been relatively silent about sex, other than to tut or frown when they see practices of which they don't approve. Or worse still, they don't think the Bible is that interested in the subject. Writing in her influential, but secular, 2020 book *Why Sex Doesn't Matter*, psychologist Olivia Fane claims to be outraged at the way Christians want to reclaim sex: "We hurriedly scan the Bible for the good news that Jesus Christ thought of sex as deep and meaningful as we like to imagine, but he doesn't even mention it, just a few random thoughts about adulterers".

No Christian would share her casual view of the Scriptures, but deep down we might wonder if she wasn't onto something. Could it be that sex, in the end, just isn't very important? We hope we've shown you that this is not the case; that, in fact, while we live in this world and marriages continue, nothing could be further from the truth.

Others will believe that we're wrong to have spoken about sex at all. If you've made it this far in the book, it's probably not you, but perhaps there is a niggling doubt there somewhere. To an extent we've inherited an odd view of history which has relegated sexual intimacy to the bottom drawer. We've not been helped in this by the rewriting of the Victorians which has made them a byword for being anti-sex. In his historical book, *Inventing the Victorians,* researcher Matthew Sweet has shown how the archetypal sex story from the nineteenth century was nothing more than fake news. Most people have heard the one about our starchy ancestors who even covered piano and table legs to stop them turning young men on; but the story is actually an early piece of satire, like a *Private Eye* column or a piece on *Saturday Night Live* to poke fun at—of all people—buttoned-up Americans.

In fact, our Victorian forebears were eager to find out everything they could about the human body and how to make sex better. Perhaps the best example of this is the book that got banned. (No, not that one, although the story of *Lady Chatterley's Lover* reveals a similar desire.) This one was called *The Fruits of Philosophy*, written by American doctor Charles Knowlton early in the 19th century. It was a book written primarily for women to help them understand their own bodies, and to practice birth control. Reading it today is a strange experience because much of it is a collection of old wives' tales which have been largely discredited. It's nothing special.

However, the book begins by dispassionately exploring the various parts of sexual anatomy in a way which medical textbooks were shy to do: remember *Gray's Anatomy's* failure to identify the clitoris until after World War II? Well, Knowlton was telling women just where it was and what it was for, back in 1832.

The book was not published in the UK until 1876. The first man to attempt to publish it was sentenced to two years hard labour, primarily because of the birth-control section of the book, which was considered outside the bounds of healthy practice. The well-known reformer Annie Besant republished the book in March 1877 and by April she was under arrest for breaching the Obscene Publications Act. This time it was the established church pushing for her arrest, again because of the birth-control sections of the book.

Between publication and arrest (just a couple of weeks), the book sold in its thousands. In its first 20 minutes of sale, hundreds of copies were purchased. People wanted to know about their bodies. People wanted sex to be better. So it has always been.

In fact, if anything we may be the ones that are unusual. Our society is extraordinarily permissive about sex while, at the same time, presiding over declining rates of sexual activity. This strange and unique combination sets *us* apart from those who have gone before, not the other way around. This is the moment for Christians to say, "We believe in something better".

A POSITIVE MESSAGE

God's plan for married couples is to enjoy sexual intimacy together, not simply for what it produces (children) but for what it signifies (union with Christ) and therefore what it brings to us as couples (closeness). The intimacy we enjoy is foundational to marriage—a holy gift from a gracious God. It is for us to serve each other. It is for us to enjoy each other. It is for us to learn about and from each other.

All of which means it is also something in which we should long to make progress. This is our goal, our *end*: longing for sexual sanctification; not that sex needs to be more frequent (although it may); nor that sex needs to be more varied (though it may); nor even that sex needs to be more ambitious (though it may); but that sex for married Christians ought to be more *meaningful*. It ought to be holier. And holier sex will be better sex. And better sex will bring us *closer*.

The Bible principles we have established will help with this. But there is no substitute for talking and praying it through, and taking steps forward together. We've deliberately not answered every question nor even given stock answers for the ones we have tackled. Your questions are for you to answer on your own. Don't confuse privacy with indifference—just because these are conversations that no one else will see you having, don't assume it doesn't matter if you don't bother.

If you believe in the gospel and if you believe in growth in godliness, then what are you waiting for?

So, over to you.

And please could you shut the door before you begin.

APPENDIX 1

I'VE SUFFERED SEXUAL ABUSE IN THE PAST

Make no mistake: sexual abuse is evil and its effects ugly, long-lasting and sometimes overwhelming. It's also much more prevalent than we might care to imagine. Christian writers Justin and Lindsay Holcomb have taken a strong interest in this issue. They reckon that "one in four women and one in six men are or will be victims of sexual assault in their lifetime". So, while this is not a book about sexual abuse, we must—as part of setting out a vision for holy, healthy and fulfilled sexual intimacy—say a little about how sexual abuse might affect a godly marriage. In this short section, we can only offer some very initial gospel solutions for what is often a very complex issue.

We don't mean to trivialise the issue by only dealing with it briefly; instead, by talking about it *at all* we want to show you that, as it matters to you, it matters to us, and it matters to others too. We want to help you move towards healing your very deep scars. We will also suggest one or two places where you might find further help.

LET'S BE HONEST ABOUT THE REALITY OF SEXUAL ABUSE

Understandably, those who have suffered this terrible cruelty often find it hard to face up to their painful experiences. For some it will be a very private secret, perhaps one that has never been mentioned to anyone else. For others, the hurts will be so deep that they will be living in a state of confusion—with emotions ranging from denial ("It didn't really happen") on one end of the scale, through to shame and guilt ("It's all my fault") on the other. These reactions are perfectly normal and perfectly understandable.

If the statistics quoted above are right, it's probable that at least some people reading this book will themselves be someone, or married to someone, who is a victim. If the psychologists are right, then it's also possible that—if your partner is the victim—they may not have told you or had great difficulty in telling you about it. If so, then we urge you, do not be quick to judge. You should not see it as a failure, on your partner's part, to be honest and frank with you. Rather, it is all part of the ugliness and damage caused by sexual abuse.

For sure, there are some who want to stick their heads in the sand and say, "Surely the problem is overstated". Or "It's not likely to happen to Christians". If that is you, then we urge you to simply flick through the pages of Genesis. This is not a new phenomenon. In his book, *The Genesis of Sex*, Bible commentator O. Palmer Robertson sets out the impact that the entry of sin into God's perfect world has on sexual relationships. He argues that, right from the beginning, the effect is comprehensive: carelessness, lust, adultery, rape, incest and homosexuality are all clearly present in just the first book of the Bible. Though we must never lose our ability to be shocked by sin, we must not be surprised by it.

Perhaps what makes sexual abuse seem more prevalent today is that we are more open to talking about the reality of sexual abuse and the impact that it has on individuals and relationships. While such talk is immensely painful, this openness is a good step forward. And the openness needs to begin by freely admitting that the effects of abuse may be long lasting. These effects can be varied: spiritual, emotional, physical or perhaps a bewildering combination of all three. In particular, they may make healthy, happy sex difficult for a married couple. *Closer* may seem elusive.

Is there any hope? Is the situation too bleak to resolve? It is true, we must be realistic when it comes to the damage that sexual abuse can cause. A "stick your head in the sand" approach will not serve those who have been abused themselves, nor those married to them. But just as we must be realistic about abuse, we must also be realistic about the gospel, which is good news for the whole of our lives.

LET'S BE REALISTIC ABOUT THE HOPE OF THE GOSPEL

The good news of the salvation held out to us in the gospel of Jesus Christ is that God himself has waged war on sin and its effects—and won! As the Holcombs put it in their book, "The cross is God's attack on sin and violence". We also need to know that the redemption God graciously gives us is total: spiritual, emotional and physical. We are whole beings, made in God's image, and our renewal is also of our whole beings. One day we shall be transformed into the likeness of Christ to spend an eternity with him where there will be "no more death or mourning or crying or pain, for the old order of things has passed away" (Revelation 21 v 4).

There is a two-fold challenge for those who have suffered sexual abuse, and for those ministering to them. First, there is the challenge to believe that the gospel is comprehensive in this way. Most of us have grown up hearing that God in Christ "forgives all your sins" (Psalm 103 v 3a), but we are more unsure about the next few phrases…

> … and heals all your diseases, who redeems your life from the pit and crowns you with love and compassion, who satisfies your desires with good things so that your youth is renewed like the eagle's. The LORD works righteousness and justice for all the oppressed.   Psalm 103 v 3b-6

Can this really be true? Where is the healing for victims? So often it seems absent. Where is the renewal for those who are dejected? So often, it seems elusive. Where is the justice for those who have been abused? So often, it seems absent. Perhaps you are struggling to believe that the death of Christ could be so comprehensive?

To this challenge we must add a second connected one: that of timing. If the redemption God offers is total, why can't we experience it all now? Surely, if our sins are forgiven *today*, then I can ask and rely upon God to deliver healing, renewal and justice just as immediately?

The reality of the gospel is that we have to be patient to wait for the final redemption of our whole selves. This is even true when it comes to sin. We know we are forgiven now, but we continue to feel the effects of sin, both in terms of ongoing temptation and also in the consequences of sins we or others may have committed. It should not surprise us, therefore, that the effect of our redemption in other areas requires the same patience. But the timing does not affect the reality. Just because we do not experience the total redemption Christ has won for us now, does not make it any less real or certain. It is this reality and certainty that all Christians must hold onto, and especially those who have suffered, or are caring for those who have suffered, sexual abuse.

Moreover, the reality for those who have embraced the gospel is one of sanctification—there is progress to be made in this life. We all experience this when it comes to sin and its effect in our lives and we should not be surprised when we begin to enjoy some of the benefits of redemption that await us here and now. So, though it can be a slow and painful process, we know of couples who will testify that there has been a measure (and an increasing measure) of spiritual, physical and emotional healing following abuse, even though they know full redemption is still in the future.

Indeed, it is this hope for the future that allows all Christians to rely on God for the present and trust him to do a gracious work in us, as we come to terms with the evils of abuse.

Wonderfully, in a marriage, God gives us a partner to support us, pray for and with us, and encourage us in this difficult journey. We are never alone, as God lives in us in the person of his Spirit. And as married couples he has graciously given us a loving spouse to also walk the road to restoration.

LET'S LEARN TO TAKE THE FIRST STEPS TOGETHER

It shouldn't come as a surprise to you to learn that our same five principles are a help to journeying the healing process together. We don't apply them in exactly the same way, but as they are found in God's inspired word, they provide a great help in learning to take the first steps to recovery together. Let's consider them briefly.

Let's do it: Sexual intimacy in a marriage is a good, healthy, and holy thing. It's important for victims of sexual abuse to recover this godly view of sex. For them, sex is very often associated with shame, guilt, despair or sin. The recovery can take a long time, but it is possible to recalibrate and see sex positively and to desire our spouses sexually. The first step is to be clear that the holiness of sex depends, in some part, on the person you are having sex with. A sexual encounter might be holy or sinful, despite it taking place in the same location with the same activity. It all depends on who your partner is. Therefore, thinking about sexual intimacy in terms of the person you are making love to (or hoping to) is a good first step to healing. A sexual act that has been forced upon you by another, for example, is not in the same category as sex with a spouse. They are not both "sex" and thinking about them in that way will be unhelpful. Try using loving language to describe what couples enjoy. For example, think of "making love" or "enjoying one another" rather than the colder "sex" or any other vulgar expression.

Keep taking the tablets: Part of your recalibration needs to turn your view of sex around from seeing it as negative (harmful, abusive) to positive. Sex is preventative and—in a marriage—a good thing precisely because there is so much immorality occurring. So, though it may seem counter-intuitive, the answer to "sinful sex" is not "no sex" but "good sex". Avoiding sexual intimacy is often a short-term solution to a painful past, but it is not a medium-term solution, because loving, wholesome sex is the very thing God has given us to battle the immorality in the world.

It's not about you: The principle of the selflessness of married sex is helpful for both those who are married to sexual-abuse victims and those who are victims themselves. For those married to victims, perhaps eager to enjoy sex within marriage, you must always be thinking about how you can help and serve your partner. Loving patience may be required.

For victims, we want to lovingly say that part of the road to recovery is to rediscover the joy of serving your partner with the sexual intimacy you can offer him or her. When you've had something bad done *to you*, it is in learning that you have something beautiful to offer someone else that you can take the first steps to redemption.

Let's talk about it: Couples need to be honest and open with each other about sexual abuse. That is an easy sentence for us to write, but a very difficult one for you to act upon. There are all kinds of reasons why victims don't want to talk about abuse or even acknowledge it, even to those very close to them. Nevertheless, having a partner who loves and cherishes us provides a loving setting for openness, tears and recovery. It may take a long time, but healing is possible, and God has brought you together to be a one-flesh union; so do not ignore his providence.

Keep the door closed: We have been careful thus far to set out the privacy of sexual intimacy. What happens between you is just between you. We did suggest, however, back when we introduced this principle, that there may be certain circumstances where outside help is needed. This may be one. Such help does not destroy the privacy of intimacy. You are not inviting anybody else to share it. Instead, you are recognising that God has placed you in a local and wider community of believers and sometimes it is wholly appropriate to seek help from others.

We are fully aware that in the midst of the pain and suffering that sexual abuse creates, our answers could seem very trite. There are no easy solutions and we do not mean to trivialise the difficulties in recovering from abuse of any kind. Nevertheless, we are also confident in the power of God and the inspiration of Scripture. So we invite you to prayerfully and carefully learn to take the first steps to healing.

FURTHER READING

If you, your partner or someone you know has suffered sexual abuse, then we recommend Justin and Lindsey Holcomb's excellent book *Rid of My Disgrace: Help and Healing for Victims of Sexual Assault* (Crossway, 2011). For those walking with victims, DayOne have an excellent little booklet called *Help! Someone I Love Has Been Abused*. Although it's about a slightly different subject, Helen Thorne's book *Walking With Domestic Abuse Sufferers* (IVP, 2018) offers some biblical and thoughtful strategies for helping those who are suffering.

There are many good secular organisations that also support victims of sexual abuse. In the UK, these are grouped together under an umbrella organisation called The Survivors Trust.

In the US, there are many different organisations that can help but a good place to start is the Administration for Children and Families website (part of the US Department of Health and Human Services). Their webpage contains some useful links: www.acf.hhs.gov/trauma-toolkit/victims-of-sexual-abuse.

Above all, we pray you will have the courage to be able to talk and pray together about what has happened to you and seek the help you both need to let the gospel heal the deep wounds you have unjustly suffered.

APPENDIX 2

I'M DEALING WITH PAST SEXUAL SIN

Two members of our extended family (a mother and daughter) once appeared in a double page spread in the *Daily Mail*, a large-circulation tabloid newspaper in the UK. What set them apart to receive this kind of attention? It was not some random act of heroism, nor a noble battle against all the odds. Rather, it was the news that both had kept themselves pure for their wedding day. They were both virgins as they walked down the aisle. It was a generous article, but the very fact it was included in the first place screamed out, "How weird is this!"

According to the US National Survey of Reproductive and Contraceptive Knowledge in 2009, 42% of single 18-29-year olds who self-identified as evangelicals said they were in a sexual relationship (compared to 52% of the population as a whole). The data is probably overstated: in most US surveys, the term "evangelical" is very broad; moreover, the survey was conducted for a National Campaign Against Teen Pregnancy by a pro-abortion lobby group. These factors often skew responses.

Nevertheless, even allowing for such overstatement, the message is clear: while the vast majority of single Christians fight and win the sexual purity battle, many do not. And even for those who are successfully fighting sin and temptation in the longer term, there are moments of weakness and sin which can change things for ever: virginity once lost cannot be reclaimed. And sexual sin is not limited to penetrative intercourse. There are many other sins which can affect future intimacy, not least the increasing use of pornography as a sexual outlet.

This is simply describing the issue for Christians. We want and expect singles and couples to be converted by the good news of Jesus Christ. And we should not be surprised when there are all manner of past experiences and sins to confess. It is itself a glorious thing that men and women are saved from a lifetime of rebellion and ungodliness to serve the living God and every Christian must wrestle with the consequences of past sins impacting relationships at every level.

We wanted to write a few words to those for whom past sexual sin of this kind is now holding them back in enjoying the intimacy that God gives in Christian marriage. We can't address every issue, but we want to show how the gospel of Jesus Christ allows us to be honest, brings healing and offers hope. Along the way you will see how each of our five principles is brought to bear, though we will not address them in order.

THE GOSPEL DEMANDS HONESTY

It is impossible to believe the good news of salvation without being honest with ourselves. The extraordinary reality of the gospel is that the death of Christ Jesus covers over all our sins— with no exceptions. The sinner who comes to the cross with true repentance receives forgiveness and the promise that "as far as the east is from the west, so far has he removed our transgressions from us" (Psalm 103 v 12). True repentance demands that we are honest about our failings. The sinner who is in denial about his or her sin or thinks that sin doesn't matter to God, has failed to grasp the reality of the gospel and cannot be truly repentant.

In a marriage, this honesty needs to extend to your spouse. It is a Bible principle that we are to "confess [our] sins to each other" (James 5 v 16). Quite how this is interpreted in the Christian church has been a subject of much debate over the centuries, but in a marriage it cannot mean less than being honest with your spouse. You are a one-flesh unit, individually made by God and brought together by him. This is *Let's talk about it* in action. A marriage cannot—we believe—be healthy and fulfilled if couples are deliberately keeping secrets from one another.

Of course, there is a wisdom call as to how much needs to be shared. If a husband, perhaps before he was converted, had multiple sexual partners, it may be that the wife does not need every detail. But the principle is still the same: there are sins to confess to God and to your spouse—recognising that your sin has deeply affected them too.

In a brief response to a question about sex before marriage, pastor and author John Piper explains this lucidly, saying that a spouse must be prepared to say to his or her partner, "I failed you. I failed God and I am deeply, deeply sorry. I hate what I did. I hate the hurt it caused you and me… I hate the disrespect I showed you…"

Such an attitude reflects another of our principles: *It's not about you.* In any Christian relationship, confessing our sins to one another and seeking forgiveness is a necessary part of recognising that we have deep obligations and commitments to those to whom we are joined by the unifying gospel of Jesus Christ. This is—in part—what Paul means by "make every effort to keep the unity of the Spirit" (Ephesians 4 v 3). We should always be thinking how our words, attitudes and actions affect others, and when they do so negatively, seek to remedy any hurt we cause. The loss of virginity, for example, or a porn addiction, has given to someone else something that God has determined you should keep for a spouse. By pursuing either of these (or other sexual sins) we are robbing our loved one of what is rightfully theirs, and therefore breaching the principle we have established.

There is one final principle to apply here: *Keep the door closed.* Sexual sins are real and damaging and must be confessed, but this is not a public event. It may be that you need to seek help to recover from the effects of sexual sin, but for the most part the action of confession and restoration is a private one. It doesn't need to feature on the church meeting agenda, nor the home-group prayer list. In your marriage, confess your sins to each other—that's your starting point.

THE GOSPEL BRINGS HEALING

James' injunction about confession comes with a promise. "Confess your sins to each other and pray for each other *so that you may be healed*" (our emphasis). The context is quite tricky; the command comes in a difficult section of James' letter dealing with faith and healing, and it is almost certain that James does not have in mind the emotional scars that are left by sexual sin.

Nevertheless, the principle is a broad Bible one. God forgives and restores and brings healing too. This healing is not always immediate; indeed, it sometimes takes a long time. Nevertheless, the promise of healing is real and the Spirit is powerful to bring peace, comfort and restoration.

Part of this healing is to recognise that there are two kinds of sex: holy sex and unholy sex. Context is everything. Sleeping with a wife or husband and sharing sexual intimacy with them is ordained by God to do us good and be pleasing to him, as well as to us. This is *Let's do it* in action. But the very same act outside of marriage (even with the same person) fits into a different category all together. It is sin. It is unholy—displeasing to God and rightly deserving of his righteous anger.

Realising this truth is a necessary step to repentance, of course, but it is also a necessary step to healing. Such healing does not come from abstinence. The answer to unholy sex is not no-sex-at-all. Rather, the answer to unholy sex is holy intimacy. It is to recover the purpose and joy that God intended sexual intimacy to have in its proper context and allowing that to define your future.

THE GOSPEL ALLOWS US TO HOPE

Such gospel optimism allows us to hope for better things in the future. Gospel honesty allows us to be realistic about the pain and hurt that has been caused. Gospel healing allows us to believe that God can redeem even the darkest of situations. And gospel hope allows us to anticipate that it is possible to recover the full delight of sexual intimacy that God purposes for married couples.

Previous sexual experience before marriage is not, in and of itself, a barrier to good enjoyment. There are some rare instances where it is not sinful. For example, two people who have been widowed and then marry will bring all kinds of past experiences and history to a marriage. This has to be worked through and can result in a new delight in intimacy. There's nothing wrong about their past or their present. God endorses their union as holy and there are not sexual sins from the past to confess.

It is good to point this out, not to excuse any sin you may have yourselves given in to, but to show that past sexual experience can be redeemed and a couple, pursuing the path of holiness, can find full enjoyment and delight in every aspect of their marriage, including in the bedroom. They can discover that far from being sinful, sex in a marriage is about preventing sin (*Keep taking the tablets*).

It is neither trite nor unrealistic to allow ourselves to hope in this way. Perhaps if any change were dependent upon our own abilities or emotional reserves, then we would be right to be pessimists. But the hope of change and renewal is dependent upon the mighty Spirit of God, not upon our own miserable weakness, so we can instead describe ourselves as joyful optimists, even when the hurts are very deep.

BOOKS AND
OTHER RESOURCES

Recommending a large number of books to take you further goes against the thrust of our argument in this book—we have given you some biblical tools to apply to the questions you may have. Nevertheless, there are a few books which are useful, and cover material we have not attempted to include.

Two excellent books which set a Christian view of sex in the context of the wider world are Sam Allberry's *Why Does God Care Who I Sleep With?* (The Good Book Company, 2020) and, for a deeper analysis, Glynn Harrison's *A Better Story* (IVP, 2016).

If, like us, you missed out on any kind of decent sex education, then Australian Christian sexologist Patricia Weerakoon has written *The Best Sex for Life* (Growing Faith/Anglican Youthworks, 2013). It is a great "facts of life" book—comprehensive yet straightforward.

For those right at the start of marriage, Amelia and Greg Clarke's honeymooner's book *One Flesh* (Matthias Media, 2001) is almost 20 years old but cannot be beaten.

For a more theological view of the place of sex in God's creation there is the basic *And Then He Knew Her* written by us (Christian Focus, 2015) or, for a more thorough analysis, we recommend *What is the Meaning of Sex?* (Crossway, 2013) by Denny Burk.

We have said little about the "putting off" that is part of our sexual sanctification. However, two titles we like are *Sexual Sanity for Men* by David White (New Growth Press, 2012) and its corresponding volume *Sexual Sanity for Women* (New Growth Press, 2013) by Ellen Dykas.

People are always asking us what is our favourite marriage book. We want to convince you that you are your own best marriage book. Talk about it. Read and reflect on Scripture. Pray. And step forward in confident faith.

But if you want a book to read together, we think it's best to ask someone you trust in your church—perhaps one of the leaders. What would they recommend? There are so many options; on the whole, stick to well-known and trustworthy authors.

BIBLIOGRAPHY

These are all the titles we have referenced directly in our book, apart from the appendices. They are not necessarily recommendations.

Sam Allberry, *Why Does God Care Who I Sleep With?* (The Good Book Company, 2020).

Nina Brochmann and Ellen Stokken Dahl, *Wonder Down Under* (Yellow Kite, 2019).

Douglas Brown, *Just Do It* (Crown Publishing, 2010).

Don Carson, *For the Love of God Volume 1* (Crossway, 2006).

L. M. Coleman and R. Ingham, "Exploring Difficulties" in *Health Education Research*, Vol 14, Issue 6, Dec 1999.

François Giuliani *et al,* "Premature Ejaculation, a European observational study" in *European Urology*, Vol 53, Issue 5, May 2008.

Suzi Godson, *The Sex Book* (Cassell, 2002).

Glynn Harrison, *A Better Story* (IVP, 2017).

Dave Harvey, *I Still Do* (Baker Books, 2020).

Tom Holland, *Dominion* (Little & Brown, 2019).

Adam Jones, David Robinson and Ryan Seedall, "The Role of Sexual Communication" in *Journal of Marital & Family Therapy*, October 2017.

Kevin Leman, *Under the Sheets* (Revell, 2009).

Charla Muller, *365 Nights* (Berkley, 2008).

O. Palmer Robertson, *The Genesis of Sex* (P&R, 2002).

David Spiegelhalter, *Sex by Numbers* (Wellcome Collection, 2015).

Matthew Sweet, *Inventing the Victorians* (Faber & Faber, 2002).

BIBLICAL | RELEVANT | ACCESSIBLE

At The Good Book Company, we are dedicated to helping Christians and local churches grow. We believe that God's growth process always starts with hearing clearly what he has said to us through his timeless word—the Bible.

Ever since we opened our doors in 1991, we have been striving to produce Bible-based resources that bring glory to God. We have grown to become an international provider of user-friendly resources to the Christian community, with believers of all backgrounds and denominations using our books, Bible studies, devotionals, evangelistic resources, and DVD-based courses.

We want to equip ordinary Christians to live for Christ day by day, and churches to grow in their knowledge of God, their love for one another, and the effectiveness of their outreach.

Call us for a discussion of your needs or visit one of our local websites for more information on the resources and services we provide.

Your friends at The Good Book Company

thegoodbook.com | thegoodbook.co.uk
thegoodbook.com.au | thegoodbook.co.nz
thegoodbook.co.in